Nothing but Wickedness

The Delusions of Our Culture

THEODORE DALRYMPLE

London

GIBSON SQUARE

This edition published for the first time by Gibson Square in 2025

UK   Tel: +44 (0)20 7096 1100
US   Tel: +1 646 216 9813

      info@gibsonsquare.com
      gibsonsquare.com

Papers used by Gibson Square are natural, recyclable products made from wood grown in sustainable forests; inks used are vegetable based. Manufacturing conforms to ISO 14001, and is accredited to FSC and PEFC chain of custody schemes. Colour-printing is through a certified CarbonNeutral® company that offsets its CO2 emissions.

Contents

Nothing but Wickedness   9

1   Irredeemable   15
2   Death an Evil   36
3   Sanity   48
4   Intoxication   58
5   Addiction   68
6   Dictators   81
7   Ideas   93
8   Sic Transit   124
9   Shakespeare   142
10 Gloria Mundi   161
11 Imagination   172

Reality   188

'In making an estimate, therefore, of the miseries that arise from the disorders of the body, we must consider how many diseases proceed from our own laziness, intemperance, or negligence; how many the vices or follies of our ancestors have transmitted to us; and beware of imputing to God, the consequences of luxury, riot, and debauchery.'

Samuel Johnson, *Sermon 5*

Nothing but wickedness

Dr Samuel Johnson (1709-1784) had many illnesses, and even more ascribed to him by writers, but he had a strong constitution and lived to what was, for the time, an old age. He was interested in physic and was willing to experiment on himself. On his deathbed, frustrated by the inability of his doctors to relieve the gross oedema of his legs, he cut deeply into his own flesh.

Johnson, whom Voltaire (wrongly) called a superstitious dog, believed that science would help to relieve mankind of much misery, but not of misery as such. Living at a time when poverty meant not an income lower than 60% of the median income but having little to eat and rags to wear, it was perhaps prescient of him to realise that, notwithstanding the horrors of poverty that he never underestimated, material progress would not mean full and final happiness.

A religious man, or perhaps (better) a man striving to keep his religious belief intact, one of his preoccupations was the problem of how an infinitely wise, powerful, knowing, and benevolent God could permit such suffering in the world. Among the great causes of suffering, of course, were disease and illness. When Johnson was writing his great *Rambler, Idler,* and *Adventurer* essays, half of all children in London died before their fifth birthday, and the city was so unhealthy that its population grew only because of migration from the countryside. The search for good health is not a cause of mass migration.

In one of his lay sermons, Johnson tackled the question of how much suffering was attributable to God's will. He wrote:

In making an estimate, therefore, of the miseries that arise from the disorders of the body, we must consider how many diseases proceed from our own laziness, intemperance, or negligence; how many the vices or follies of our ancestors have transmitted to us; and beware of imputing to God, the consequences of luxury, riot, and debauchery. There are, indeed, distempers which no caution can secure us from, and which appear to be more immediately the strokes of heaven; but these are not of the most painful or lingering kind; they are for the most part acute and violent, and quickly terminate, either in recovery or death; and it is always to be remembered, that nothing but wickedness makes death an evil.

The last sentence makes sense, of course, only if there is a future state of being whose felicities are handed out according to our desert in this life; and perhaps pedantically inclined philosophers might say that otherwise it is not death itself that is an evil, but only the truncation of existence that might have been more prolonged and is foregone by the intervention of death.

Be that as it may, I confess that whenever I read the first sentence of the part of the sermon that I have quoted, I think of the mass public drunkenness that foolish or perhaps corrupt governments have assiduously encouraged, promoted, and benefited from. What better illustration of Johnson's point could there be than that, at the last count known to me, 70% of attendances at casualty departments between midnight and 5 am are attributable in one way or another to drunkenness?

All in the mind?

There is no pleasure greater than to denounce the wickedness of the times, and since the times are always wicked the pleasure is inexhaustible.

The Reverend Jeremy Collier MA (1650-1726) was a great denouncer of the wickedness of his times. He was famous for it; in fact, it was his metier. He did not think the Glorious Revolution was glorious and refused to swear allegiance to the new monarchs, William and Mary, and he was particularly against the degeneracy and vulgarity of Restoration comedy, which he denounced in his *Short View of the Immorality and Profaneness of the English Stage*, published in 1698. He was answered in kind by Vanbrugh and Congreve, whom he especially attacked, and he wrote a riposte to their riposte. It was all good clean fun.

He also wrote a series of moral essays, many in the form of a dialogue, some of medical interest. For example, his 'A Moral Essay of Pain' takes up the question of the nature and utility of pain in a world ruled by divine providence. He defines pain as 'an unacceptable Notice arising from some Disorder in the Body.' He goes on:

> *When the Continuity of the Organ is disjoyn'd, the Nerves discomposed, and the Muscles forced into a foreign Situation; when there's a stop of the Spirits, when the Parts don't keep their Ranks, but are beaten out of the Figure which Nature has drawn them up in; then the Mind immediately receives a grating Information of what has happen'd; Which Intelligence is more or less troublesome in Proportion to the Disadvantages of the Accident.*

As any good moralist must, he points out that much pain is the fault of the sufferers themselves, a kind of punishment of their own conduct and a good lesson to them:

> *For instance, a Man of Choler and Conceit takes fire at an insignificant Affront, rushes into a Quarrel, has his Head broke, and it may be his limbs raked, into the Bargain; now when a Wound is thus impertinently made, ought it not to put the patient to some Trouble? He that's thus prodigal of his Person, and makes his Limbs serve in an ill Cause, ought to meet with a Mortification; The Punishment is but a just return for the Pride, and the Smart, it may be, the best Cure for the Folly.'*

Where indeed would our casualty departments be, what work would they have to do, were it not for those who are 'thus prodigal of their Person'?

Collier is not so fanatic as to fail to recognise that pain is sometimes undeserved, that it afflicts the righteous as well as the unrighteous; but he is particularly exercised by the fact that a person's psychological state affects the degree of pain that they feel, from which he concludes that pain, notwithstanding his initial definition of it, is not really physical at all. He refers to the fact that the barbarian Gauls, fighting the Romans, hardly felt their wounds but were abject cowards in the face of disease; whereas with 'the Grecians' it was the other way round. He gives many other examples, from the Bible and classical literature.

So pain for Collier is both physical and psychological. In a surprising way, therefore, he is a forerunner of Melzack and Wall's 'gate' theory of pain: that nerves that don't transmit pain can interfere with signals from pain nerves and inhibit the perception of pain.

His dialogue 'Of Drunkenness, between the Toper Oenophilus and the Sober Eucratius' is also of surprisingly contemporary relevance. When Oenophilus points out that people often drown their sorrows in drink, Eucratius replies: 'To throw one World after another, is a Dismal Relief against Poverty.'

Inscribe it in Whitehall, say I.

The riot of our mind

Every month for nearly six years, Johnson's biographer James Boswell (1740-1795) wrote an essay for the *London Magazine* under the name of The Hypochondriack. By hypochondriack, Boswell meant not the man who is consumed by fear of illnesses he does not have but the one who suffers from melancholy, spleen, or 'the vapours'.

If Boswell were writing his essays today, I suppose it would be as The Depressive, and he would long ago have been put on antidepressants. In issue 39, he describes the hypochondriack's symptoms:

His opinion of himself is low and desponding. His temporary dejection makes his faculties seem quite feeble. His fancy roves over the variety of characters whom he knows in the world ... and they seem all better than his own. He regrets his ever having attempted distinction and excellence in any way, because the effect of his former exertions now serves only to make his insignificance more vexing to him. Nor has he any prospect of more agreeable days when he looks forward. There is a cloud as far as he can perceive, and he supposes it will be charged with thicker vapour, the longer it continues. He is distracted between indolence and shame… He acts like a slave, not animated by inclination, but goaded by fear.

He hoped to ward off his own tendency to this condition, or these conditions, by his literary exertions.

Inauspiciously, perhaps, his first essay in the series was dated November, and he quotes a French novel that starts with the line (one wants to read on), 'In the gloomy month of November, when the people of England begin to hang and drown themselves…'

Boswell proposes two remedies to the hypochondriac: therapy, and or psychopharmacology.

The therapy is religious belief:

By religion, the Hypochondriack will have his mind fixed upon one invariable object of veneration, will have his troubled thoughts calmed by the consideration that he is here in a state of trial, that to contribute his part in carrying out the plan of providence in this state of being is his duty, and that his sufferings however severe will be found beneficial to him in the other world.

The psychopharmacological remedy Boswell proposes is drink:

To be sure we know that an excess in wine which alone can move a thick melancholy, will probably make us worse when its violent operation has ceased, so that it is in general better to bear the mental malady with firmness. Yet I am not so sure but when the black distress has been of long continuance, it may be allowable to try by way of a desperate remedy, as poisons are sometimes given in medicine, what a joyous shock will produce. To have the mind fairly disengaged from its baneful foe, even for a little while, is of essential consequence. For it may then exert its latent vigour, and… be able to get the better of what pressed it down before in abject submission.

And then come immortal words, in direct opposition to the health and safety view of human existence, which are more salient today than when they were written: 'But we are not to consider the world as an immense hospital: and whenever we see a company with wine circulating amongst them, to think that they are patients swallowing a necessary potion.'

Risk factors can seriously damage your peace of mind.

1. Irredeemable

Inside stories

Progress, it goes without saying, is not entirely uniform. Indeed, retrogression sometimes occurs, for example in the style of official prose. Where now it employs neologisms, euphemisms, and acronyms to the point of incomprehensibility, it was once clear, vigorous, and even a model for aspiring writers. Of course, in those days its authors were not so ashamed of what they did that they had to disguise it by the use of opaque language; barbarous locutions conceal a bad conscience.

Can anyone conceive of reading a contemporary official report with pleasure in its literary qualities? Having come across it by chance, I read the *Report of the Commissioners Appointed to Inquire into the Condition and Treatment of the Prisoners Confined in Birmingham Borough Prison, and the Conduct, Management and Discipline of the Said Prison,* published in 1854, not only with interest but in pleasure at the vigour of the prose, written by the three commissioners, one of whom, William Baly, was a doctor.

The inquiry was set up when a 15 year old boy committed suicide, and rumours of hideous mistreatment of prisoners became persistent. The governor, Lieutenant William Austin, RN, was a ferocious disciplinarian who introduced such innovations as the crank for hard labour (to be turned by the prisoner 10,000 times a day, or else he would be given only bread and water) and a special punishment jacket, a straitjacket with the addition of a leather hoop for the refractory prisoner's neck that was stapled to the wall.

The report was particularly damning of the prison's medical

officer, Mr J H Blount. Its conclusion about him was unequivocal: he practised 'with little regard to common decency, to say nothing of the humanity which should be exercised in a Christian country.' Even the evidence that he gave to the commissioners was criticised: 'We are bound also to express our opinion, with respect both to Lieut[enant] Ustin and to Mr Blount, that much of their evidence was given in an evasive, disingenuous and discreditable manner.'

Among Mr Blount's methods was the use of salt as a tranquilliser:

In July 1852, a prisoner of the name of Samuel Hunt, who there is great reason to believe laboured under partial insanity, having been violent, and struck or threatened to strike a warder, was by order of the governor put into a strait jacket by two of the prison officers. While they were putting it on him he was in a very excited state, resisted, endeavoured to bite, shouted, and made use of obscene language. The governor and surgeon were present. The latter directed that salt should be sent for. Salt was brought, and the surgeon, in the governor's presence, whenever the prisoner opened his mouth to shout or to bite, thrust into it a quantity of salt, repeating the proceeding until the prisoner was subdued, and became quiet.

Mr Blount believed that most epileptics were faking it and had buckets of cold water poured over them to prove it. One of them treated in this fashion died the same night of what sounds like status epilepticus.

I was reminded of my early days working in a prison. I had entered the cell of a prisoner in the company of an officer, supposedly also a nurse, when the prisoner fell to the floor in a grand mal seizure.

'Don't you do that in front of the doctor!' said the officer to the convulsing patient.

Unflattering Nightingale

We all love heroes and heroines, but even more so do we enjoy the exposure of their hidden faults. I will not speculate on why this should be so: perhaps it is that, our lives being mediocre, we fear to contemplate unmitigated the heights of human accomplishment.

The greater is the reputation; the more guiltily delicious is the debunking. When I was a child, Florence Nightingale was an untouchable heroine, like Elizabeth Fry. Before her, nurses were Dickens' Mrs Gamp; after her, they were ministering angels. Soldiers were eternally kissing her shadow as she went by.

One of the great works of historical debunking is F B Smith's *Florence Nightingale: Reputation and Power*, published in 1982. Smith, an Australian historian, sometimes makes you laugh out loud (and not because of any witticism of Miss Nightingale's). You know what you are in for from the first sentence:

> *Florence Nightingale's first chance to deploy her talent for manipulation came in August 1853. Within a short space, one learns that the Lady with the Lamp was a consummate liar: Miss Nightingale's account of her good works at the Middlesex Hospital constitute a memorable example of her powers as a titillating fabulist.*

Reflecting on the fact that Nightingale dismissed most of the staff that she herself had chosen at the first institution that she ever ran, The Invalid Gentlewoman's Institution in Harley Street, Smith says, 'The superintendent [does] not seem to have excelled in picking and training staff.' Detailing her unfair criticisms of the committee of that institution, Smith does point out her superiority in one respect: 'But none of them matched the force and ingenuity she brought to intrigue.'

This is all good, clean, knockabout fun. Some of Smith's evidence does show his subject in a lurid light—for example, her taking to task of her great bureaucratic assistant, Sidney Herbert, during his final illness, for not trying hard enough to help her, while she at the time luxuriated in the role of invalid that she was successfully to play for a further 50 years.

As is well known, Miss Nightingale rejected the germ theory of disease, arguing that, if accepted, it would impair her sanitary work. She insisted to the end of her days on dirt and miasma as the cause of disease, rejecting contagion altogether; she opposed smallpox vaccination in India; and she never grasped that the germ theory of disease was actually compatible with sanitary reform.

She was what would now be called a brilliant spin doctor. When

Agnes Jones sought admission to the Nightingale School, Florence wrote, '[Her] peculiar character is want of character.' But when Jones died in harness in Liverpool Workhouse, having after all trained at the Nightingale School, Florence turned her for propaganda purposes into a paragon.

Smith chronicles her manipulations, deviousness, evasions, and lies, but he admits that, overall, she did an immense amount of good. His aim is to disabuse us of the romantic idea that people who do good must themselves be good, but let us hope that his readers do not take this as a licence actually to be bad.

His explanation as to why Miss Nightingale did not destroy documentation that was unflattering to her memory is memorable:

> *Florence Nightingale, like Mr Richard Nixon and his tapes, was so possessed of the habit of deceit and the conviction that the full record would compel posterity to vindicate all her actions, that she could not bring herself to destroy material which had become part of her identity. Having brazened out lies in life she would brazen them out in death.*

The price of incompetence

We are inclined to suppose that our contemporary problems and discontents are entirely new and unprecedented, but when we look into the records we come to precisely the opposite, and no doubt equally unwarranted, conclusion: that there is nothing new under the sun.

Malpractice suits, for example, are not new. In 1870 the man who was to become the first professor of orthopaedic surgery in the United States, Lewis A Sayre (1820-1900), was sued by the parents of Margaret Walsh, a little girl on whom he operated in 1868. He published at his own expense the proceedings of the trial, which vindicated him, under the title *The Alleged Malpractice Suit of Walsh v Sayre.*

The little girl aged 6 was brought to him by her mother with something wrong with her hip. He diagnosed an abscess, inserted a trocar and cannula, and then opened the abscess with a scalpel, whereupon about of pint of pus spurted out to a distance of two feet

(60 cm). He then poured some carbolic into the wound, whereupon the child cried out; the mother, alarmed, snatched the child up and ran out with her. She did not return for follow-up, as Dr Sayre suggested, and sued him instead. She alleged that she had brought the child only for examination, not operation, and that the operation had in any case been negligently performed, allegedly opening the capsule of the joint and causing the child permanent damage.

There was intrigue behind the suit. The doctor who suggested in the first place that she take her daughter to Dr Sayre, a Dr Amariah B Vaughan, also suggested that she sue him afterwards. Sayre had operated on Mr Walsh, Margaret's father, who owed Sayre $100 (a considerable sum in those days) for the operation, which Walsh had given Vaughan but which Vaughan had failed to pass on to Sayre. This was a way for Vaughan to hang on to his $100.

Vaughan was one of the witnesses for the plaintiff; it was he who said that Sayre had incised the capsule of the joint. Under cross examination, however, Vaughan was an unimpressive figure to say the least: not only was he a recently reformed drinker, but he had no medical qualifications whatsoever and refused to answer questions about his education (or lack of it). He had been the clerk at various druggists' stores, and he claimed to have read some medical textbooks—that was all. Of the anatomy of the hip he was shown to know absolutely nothing, explaining his ignorance by saying in the witness box that he was feeling too unwell to answer such questions.

Samuel Gross, professor of surgery at the Jefferson Medical College and the subject of Thomas Eakins's great painting of Gross operating, *The Gross Clinic*, wrote a congratulatory preface to Sayre's transcript of the trial: 'I sincerely congratulate you upon the successful issue of the villainous suit against you for alleged malpractice. A few more such verdicts will go far in putting a stop to such outrageous and unjustified prosecutions.'

Alas, history has decreed otherwise, and Samuel Gross unwittingly hinted at the reason why: 'It has always appeared to me that a lawyer who will permit himself to bring suit for malpractice against an honorable medical man… must be essentially a base, unprincipled man.'

But: 'Some members of the American bar are, unfortunately, too

19

prone, for the sake of a paltry fee, to encourage and engage in such prosecutions.'

I am glad to say, however, that not everything has remained the same: the fees are no longer paltry.

J Gilbert Dale's Imperatine

Few medical texts are known to me that are more poetic than two volumes published by the British Medical Association in 1909 and 1912, respectively, entitled *Secret Remedies* and *More Secret Remedies*. They were best sellers, my copy of the first being among the 105th thousand.

The BMA, irritated by the continuing success of quacks and their nostrums, decided to publish an analysis of popular remedies. As the introduction to the first volume states,

> *Care has been taken to reproduce the claims and exuberant boasts of the vendors, and the contrast between them and the list of banal ingredients which follow must strike every reader. This juxtaposition of analytical facts and advertising fancies is instructive and sometimes entertaining, the fancy is so free and the fact so simple.*

The names of the products are so wonderful that a list of them is a poem in itself. Figuroids, Fell's Reducing Treatment, Fenning's Children's Cooling Powders, Corpulin, Chameleon Oil, Alfred Cromton's Specific for Deafness, Pomies' Anti-Cataract Mixture, Antidipso (for drunkenness), Dipsocure, the Teetolia Treatment, Dr Martin's Miracletts, Mother Siegel's Curative Syrup, Burgess's Lion Ointment, Dr Van Vleck's Complete Absorptive Pile Treatment, Zam-Buk, Professor O Phelps Brown's Vervain Restorative Assimilant, Whelpton's Purifying Pills, Carter's Little Liver Pills, J Gilbert Dale's Imperatine, Jefferson Dodd's Corrective, Nurse Hammond's Improved Remedies, Mrs Stafford-Brookes' Pelloids, Baring-Gould's Anti-Rheumatic Pearls, Zox, Oquit, Bishop's Gout Varalettes, Fitzcure (for epilepsy), Dr Niblett's Vital Renewer, Ozonia, Box's Pills, and Golden Fire.

No condition was beyond the reach of secret remedies. For

example, an advertisement for Rice's Treatment for Rupture had a picture of a bricklayer filling up a hole in a wall: 'Do you see this bricklayer closing up the opening in the wall. That is the way to cure ruptures, by filling in the opening with new and stronger tissue.'

I confessed to a sneaking admiration for the ingenuity of the argument. The advertisement continues:

The break [in the tissue] may be no larger than the tip of your finger. But it is large enough to allow part of the intestines to crowd through. Of course this cannot heal unless nature is assisted. That is just what this method does. It enables you to retain the protrusion inside the wall in its proper place.

We give you a Developing Lymphol to apply to the rupture opening. This penetrates through the skin to the edges of the opening and removes the hard ring which has formed round the break.

Then the healing process begins. Nature, no longer handicapped by the protruding bowel and hardened ring at the opening, and stimulated by the action of the Lymphol, throws out her supply of lymph, and the opening is again filled with new muscle.

Isn't this simple? Isn't this reasonable? Oils of peppermint and origanum and tincture of capsicum seem to have been the main ingredients.

Sometimes the style is laudably telegraphic: 'Oh my back, how it aches! Why? Fitch's Kidney and Liver-Cooler. Trade Mark. Sluggish Liver. Inactive kidneys. Over-heated blood. Bad urine. Acts chemically by absorption.'

'Myriads of people thank Providence for Dr Var's Kidney Pills.' As for Pastor Felke's Honey Cod Liver Oil—'recommended in preference to ordinary forms on account of its pleasant taste'—it contained cod liver oil with oil of peppermint and raspberry syrup.

How strange our predecessors were, how credulous to believe the things they did. Had they never heard of real remedies, such as Hopi ear candles and coffee enemas?

The foul taste of medicine

I was one of the many middle class children whose tonsils were sacrificed to the need of ear, nose, and throat surgeons to increase their incomes. I am not in the least bitter about it because of the ice cream I was given to eat after the operation, though I did dive down to the bottom of the bed and spit out the foul tasting medicine I was also given. The ward sister rebuked me sternly for my bad behaviour, but I had my revenge when my mother gave me a box of chocolate letters that I distributed to all the staff with the conspicuous exception of her.

Medicine has always tasted foul, of course; indeed, the fouler the better. Joseph Hall, DD (1574-1656) meditated on this in one of his Occasional Meditations, which he entitled 'On a medicinal potion':

How loathsome a draught is this! How offensive, both to the eye, and to the scent, and to the taste? Yea, the very thought of it, is a kind of sickness: and, when it is once down, my very disease is not so painful for the time, as my remedy. How doth it turn the stomach, and wring the entrails; and works a worse distemper, than that, whereof I formerly complained?

Reading this, I confess, I thought of my time in a malarious country in Africa, where I recommended proguanil as prophylaxis and grew angry when my patients did not take it, though I did not take it myself because it nauseated me so. Better, I thought, malaria than a life of gastritis; and to this day, 20 years later, the very thought of it is a kind of sickness.

The Right Reverend Dr Hall expressed a general pessimism about the gustatory quality of medicines that has, on the whole, been borne out by experience: 'And yet [the potion] must be taken, for health: neither could it be / wholesome, if it were less unpleasing; neither could it make me / whole, if it did not first make me sick.'

For the good bishop, it is divinely ordained that what is good for us can only be unpleasant, at the very least a denial of our fleshly inclinations. The healthfulness of the unpleasant is a metaphor for the human condition: 'Why do I not cheerfully take, and quaff up that bitter cup of / affliction, which my wise God hath mixed for the health of my / soul?'

The reaction of Lord Bishop of Exeter (later of Norwich) to his medicine was precisely mine 50 years ago: 'Why do I then turn away my head, and make faces, and shut mine / eyes, and stop my nostrils, and nauseate and abhor to take the / harmless potion for health?'

Why, he goes on to ask, make such a fuss when 'we have seen mountebanks, to swallow dismembered toads, and drink the poisonous brother after them, only for a little ostentation and gain?'

At the time of my tonsillectomy I had a friend who used to drink the water in puddles and swallow earthworms, only for a little ostentation (to appal the adults) and gain (we paid him three pence to do it). I certainly wasn't prepared, then, to swallow foul tasting medicine for that most trivial and uncoupling of all reasons, my own good.

Crimes and misdescriptions

When I was about 12 years old, my father took me to see a production of *Measure for Measure* at Stratford. Angelo, the fanatical puritan and anti-sensualist who is left in charge when the Duke leaves Vienna for a time, and who then falls prey to an illicit passion for Isabella, which he tries by means of corruption to consummate, was played by Marius Goring.

Goring was a very distinguished actor and an accomplished linguist who played cabaret in German in Berlin and Hamlet in French in Paris. During the war, he was head of the BBC's broadcasts in German to Germany; he also was a founder of the actors' union, Equity. When he died, aged 85, more than a third of a century after I saw him in Stratford, I imagined him still clad in the burgundy velvet tunic he wore as Angelo, and still a middle-aged man: such is the egotism of the imagination. When he played Angelo, in fact, he was exactly the age (49) I was when he died; not much of a coincidence, perhaps, but so persistent is the tendency to superstition that it had a patina of significance for me.

Another coincidence, perhaps, was that Goring's father, Charles Goring, who died in 1919 (aged 49), was a prison doctor, as I was myself to become. He wrote an enormous tome, published by HMSO, called *The English Convict*, which consists of a statistical study of 3000 prisoners taken at random.

This immense work, truly a labour of Hercules, with vast numbers of tabulations correlating everything with everything else, was undertaken to refute the theories of Cesare Lombroso, the Italian doctor, anthropologist, and criminologist who believed in the existence of natural born criminals who displayed atavistic physical signs of their criminality. You could tell a criminal, more or less, by his eyes, or ears, or some other physical characteristic.

I think Goring had fun with the whole idea: 'We will now describe in detail some of the salient 'criminal characteristics,' according to the teaching of Lombroso's school. The hair of the criminal... is dark and thick, they tell us; another common type is woolly in texture; whereas red and grey hair, and baldness, are relatively rare among criminals. The head is alleged to be anomalous in shape, and in its dimensions. Dimensionally, there are two types of criminal heads: the one larger, the other smaller than the normal type. In shape, five types are described... the head of the criminal is oxy-cephalic, trigono-cephalic, scapho-cephalic, plagio-cephalic, hydro-cephalic and sub-micro-cephalic... The expression is cringing, timid, humble, suppliant; [or it is] brazen, shameless, ferocious, brutal.' And so on and so forth.

My copy of this vast work is annotated by a follower of Lombroso, to judge by the irritated pencilled comments in the margins. For example, when Dr Goring writes 'Atavistic, insane, savage, degenerate, all or any of these things, whatever they may mean, the criminal may be; one thing the criminologists will not let him be: he is not, he never is, say the Lombrosians, a perfectly normal human being,' the furious annotator (whose annotations, I note, nevertheless cease at page 27 of 440) has written 'Who is?'

The state of being ill

In the days when children were taught to write essays, they were given Charles Lamb to read. It was hoped, I suppose, that his *Essays of Elia* would impart, by a kind of literary osmosis, a grace, economy, and gentle irony to their prose.

Lamb was an amiable man who spent most of his life as a clerk at the East India Company. Although he stuttered, he was a wit. When his office superior accused him of arriving late for work he replied that, to make up for it, he left early.

He lived all his life with his sister, Mary, with whom he wrote the famous *Tales from Shakespeare*. Their domesticity, however, was often interrupted by Mary's mental illness. In 1796, Charles returned home to wrest the knife from Mary's hand with which she had just stabbed their mother to death.

The verdict at the trial was lunacy, and Mary was sent to an institution: Warburton's Private Mad-House in Hoxton, from which she was released on recovery into what I suppose we would now call the community—and to which institution she returned when she relapsed, as she often did. Warburton's Private Mad-House was later exposed as practising every possible cruelty, torture, and fraud.

Mary's illness was certainly manic depression. Lamb's earliest biographer, Thomas Noon Talfourd, gives a description of grandiosity, flight of ideas, and clang associations that could hardly be bettered, indeed could be used in textbooks:

> *Though her conversation in sanity was never marked by smartness or repartee; seldom rising beyond that of a sensible quiet gentlewoman appreciating and enjoying the talents of her friends, it was otherwise in her madness. She would fancy herself in the days of Queen Anne or George the First; and describe the brocaded dames and courtly manners, as though she had been bred among them... It was all broken and disjointed, so that the hearer could remember little of her discourse; but the fragments were like the jewelled speeches of Congreve, only shaken from their setting. There was sometimes a vein of crazy logic running through them, associating things essentially most dissimilar, but connecting them by verbal association in strange order. As a mere physical instance of deranged intellect, her condition was, I believe, extraordinary; it was as if the finest elements had been shaken into fantastic combinations like those of a kaleidoscope.*

One of Lamb's essays is called 'The Convalescent'—he himself was once admitted to a 'mad house' and had episodes of depression ever after, as well as drinking far too much—and is a wonderful description of the experience of being ill in bed.

The sick person tosses in bed, 'moulds his pillow to the ever-varying requisitions of his throbbing temples' and 'changes sides oftener than a politician.' His horizons become limited: 'How sickness enlarges the dimensions of a man's self to himself! He is his own exclusive object.' He becomes an unimaginative solipsist:

> *To the world's business he is dead. He understands not what the callings and occupations of mortals are; when the doctor makes his daily call… even in the lines on that busy face he reads no multiplicity of patients, but solely conceives of himself as the sick man. To what other uneasy couch the doctor is hastening, is no speculation which he can at present entertain.*

No one reads Lamb these days, of course.

No good deed...

When I was a small boy I picked every last bud from the red peony bushes in the garden and presented them to my father. 'Look, Daddy,' I said. 'Cherries.' I was beaten with a bamboo cane for my conscientiousness, but I have not held it against peonies.

I was reminded of this incident by the beginning of Stephen Crane's novella *The Monster*, published in 1897. Crane (1871-1900) is mostly remembered for his novel about the US civil war, *The Red Badge of Courage*.

The Monster takes place in a small town called Whilomville. At the beginning of the story, Dr Trescott's little boy, Jimmie, decapitates a peony while playing trains in the garden. Though the boy is terrified by what his father will say, Dr Trescott reacts less forcefully than did my father: but then, Jimmie removed only one bud, and accidentally, not deliberately.

One night Dr Trescott's house burns down. Henry Johnson, a black servant, heroically rescues the doctor's son from the fire, but in the process is badly burned. Dr Truscott nurses him back to life but unfortunately Henry's face 'has simply been burned away.' His neighbour, Judge Hagenthorpe, questions the doctor's decision to nurse Henry back to life: 'I am induced to say that you are performing a questionable charity in preserving this negro's life. As near as I can understand, he will hereafter be a monster, a perfect monster, and probably with an affected brain. No man can observe you and not know this was a matter of conscience with you, but I am afraid, my friend, that it is one of the blunders of virtue.' The judge then implies that Trescott should let Henry die or even help him on his way.

The doctor, though, feels an inextinguishable debt of gratitude to Henry and, after Henry pulls through, pays for him to lodge with a black family. The head of the family exploits him by keeping him as a prisoner and trying to extract a higher rate from the doctor. Henry escapes and visits old friends, but succeeds only in frightening them with his terribly maimed appearance. One small girl, whose family are patients of the doctor, falls ill from the fright. Her parents blame Dr Truscott for her illness because he has saved the life of 'the monster' who upset her.

The doctor takes Henry into his rebuilt home. From then on his practice declines. From having been the most sought after doctor in the town, he becomes the least. A delegation of prominent citizens asks him to put Henry into an institution, but the doctor refuses. The story ends with his wife crying over the teacups: none of the ladies of the town will attend her at-homes any more, and she has laid out the tea things in vain.

Crane is generally considered one of the first modern US literary realists, but of course he is also a symbolist, as all realists are. The symbolism lies in the choice of the aspect of reality that is portrayed. You don't have to know much to know what is symbolised in *The Monster*.

Diets are forever

When I was a boy my mother had a book with the title *Eat and Grow Beautiful*. As my mother was already beautiful I could not see the point of her having the book but supposed that it was because of the author's splendid name: Gayelord Hauser. For myself, I was disappointed that however much I ate I did not grow beautiful. Perhaps it was because I ate all the wrong things, such as chocolate biscuits. If I hadn't eaten so many I should have been a film star by now.

All flesh is grass, of course, but few of us are a well tended lawn.

Just how many of us are dissatisfied with ourselves, and look to food to right what nature and our previous habits have denied us, was brought home to me the other day when, at something of a loose end, I slipped into a secondhand bookshop in London. The section of diet books was larger than that devoted to economics, which proves that Doctor Johnson (as usual) was right: public affairs vex no man. We are all characters in our own soap opera.

Many of the books, as perhaps you'd expect, were written by doctors, and I took down their titles: *Life's a Bitch and then You Diet, The 30-Day Fat Burner, Diet, The Eat Right Diet, A New Way of Eating, The Harcombe Diet: Stop Counting Calories and Start Losing Weight, The Healthy Diet Calories Counter, The Green Diet, The F2 Diet, The Food Doctor Diet, Eat Yourself Slim, The Solution Beach Diet, Eat Right for Your Type, How not to Get Fat, The Wine Diet, 7 lbs in 7 Days* (the dietary equivalent of *Seven Brides for Seven Brothers*), *Neris and India's Idiot-Proof Diet, Food Combining in Thirty Days, Food Combining For Health, Food Combining Counter, Fitness on a Plate, The Ultimate New York Diet, Dr Atkins' New Diet Revolution, Margaret Fulton's Book of Slimming, The Food Doctor's Everyday Diet, The Ultimate Weight Loss Solution: the 7 Keys To Weight Loss Freedom, The End of Overeating*.

When a book's title includes words such as 'final' or 'ultimate,' there are sure to be more books to follow (how many times has the mystery of Jack the Ripper finally been solved?). The prevalence of the number seven suggests the persistence of numerological super-stition. Not surprisingly, the diet books slid by natural progression into those offering a dermatological utopia (*Younger Skin in 8 Weeks* and *The Ciminelli Solution: a 7-Day Plan for Radiant Skin*) to those offering an end to all problems whatsoever: *42 Days to Health, Wealth and Happiness; How to Make Your Dreams Come True;* and *Shortcuts to Getting a Life*.

As it happens, the bookshop was just around the corner from Harley Street, where hope of a more limited, rational, but expensive kind was on offer. But for advice on how to eat yourself slim, it was best to go round to Oxfam on Marylebone High Street.

Do authors of diet books really believe what they write? Here I remember the answer a bestselling author (and convicted confidence trickster) once gave when asked whether he believed his own theory that many human monuments had been constructed by aliens from outer space, in his strong German accent: 'The outline yes; the details no.'

Time to solve a murder case

Anticholinergics, bottles of peppermint scented aluminium hydroxide, liquorice tablets, milk diets, and vagotomy and pyloro-plasty—all the things that I remember from my childhood as treatment of peptic ulceration because my father tried them all without success (indeed, the V and P very nearly killed him)—were rendered redundant first by new pharmacological treatments and then by the discovery of the role of the *Helicobacter*.

Things have changed dramatically in other respects too. For example, in 1989, in *The Wench Is Dead*, Inspector Morse (Colin Dexter's hero of the Oxford police) was admitted with haematemesis (bleeding of the upper digestive tract), via the emergency department, to the John Radcliffe Infirmary. In those days, everything was done manually and thermometers still had mercury in them. Doctors wore white coats and the nurse in charge of a ward was a sister rather than a ward manager. However, change was in the air: the sister of the ward to which Morse was admitted, the old fashioned dragon-type, had left by the end of the book to become not the matron of another hospital, but its director of nursing services.

Once in the ward, Morse finds himself opposite an old colonel who promptly dies from septicaemia. The dead man's wife arrives later and hands round to the patients, *in memoriam*, her late husband's great work, an account of a Victorian murder. Dissatisfied with the verdict he finds in the book, Morse sets out to solve the case from his hospital bed.

The astonishing thing (from our current perspective) is that he seems to have plenty of time in which to do so. The only medical procedure to which he is ever subjected during his stay is endoscopy; whereafter he is allowed to vegetate in the ward for more than a week, and then discharged with no very great sense of urgency! Most of the other patients vegetate likewise; the man opposite him (after the death of the old colonel) seems to have little wrong with him, but his daughter who visits him is a librarian at the Bodleian who is able to help Morse with his researches into the Victorian case.

When he is not thinking about the case, Morse wanders the corridors of the hospital or completes the *Times* crossword in 10 minutes. Today, the ability to turn to the crossword page, let alone answer any of the clues, would be taken as evidence of fitness for discharge. How luxuriantly slow paced, then, were hospitals only 20 years ago.

Was it inefficiency or humanity that made them so? I recall with nostalgia a deliciously peaceful seven days in hospital in the late 1970s on my return from abroad where I had suffered heart failure from presumed viral myocarditis. I was in for investigations, but was left largely undisturbed. The ward was half empty, spotlessly clean, delightfully calm give or take the irruption of the tea trolley, and endowed with a wonderful bath of gargantuan proportions. The nurses were a sadomasochist's dream, all starch and black stockings.

Morse felt almost sad on being discharged from hospital, as I did. His stay had been a spiritual refreshment to him, as mine had been to me. True, spiritual refreshment is not what hospital is for, which perhaps is just as well since you can't measure it. In the event, also, I never got a firm diagnosis; but at least I had a personal relationship with the man who didn't make one.

Truth in the eye of the beholder

My late mother suffered a severe rash a few years before she died. She had to wait an age to consult a dermatologist, even privately, and then she saw several in swift succession. All their prescriptions made her rash much worse; the prescriptions were so bad that even stopping them did her no good.

Then she went to a homoeopath, took homoeopathic medicine for a week and recovered almost immediately. The rash melted away as the snow in sunshine. I was very pleased for her, of course, but kept a little corner of my heart free for the irritation that I felt. She, however, was delighted that there were more things in heaven and earth than are dreamt of in most doctors' philosophy.

Anton Chekhov (1860-1904) wrote an anti-homoeopathic story when he was a young man. It is called 'Malingerers,' and its protagonist is Marfa Petrovna Petchonkin, the rich widow of a general, who has practised homoeopathy as a hobby for 10 years. She is a generous hearted woman who delights in the great success she has as a healer, and often helps her patients financially when they tell her of their difficulties.

She discovers the truth when an impoverished landowner, Zamuhrishen, returns to tell her that she has cured him of the most terrible rheumatism from which he expected shortly to die. He tells her that he wasted a lot of time and money consulting ordinary doctors, who did him 'nothing but harm. They drove the disease inwards… but to drive out was beyond their science.' Zamuhrishen then levels the charge against doctors that has been levelled for centuries: 'All they care about is their fees, the brigands.'

Zamuhrishen goes down on his knees to Marfa Petrovna.

I went home from you that Tuesday, looked at the pilules that you gave me then, and wondered what good there could be in them… When I took the pilule it was instantaneous! It was as though I had not been ill, or as though it had been lifted off me. My wife looked at me with her eyes starting out of her head and couldn't believe it. 'Why, is it you, Kolya?' 'Yes, it is I,' I said. And we knelt down together before the icon, and fell to praying for our angel: 'Send her, O Lord, all that we are feeling!'

Marfa Petrovna, who is naturally delighted by the cure she has wrought, says modestly,

'It's not my doing. I am only the obedient instrument… It's really a miracle. Rheumatism of eight years' standing [cured] by one pilule of scrofuloso!'
Then Zamuhrishen tells Marfa Petrovna of his economic problems. 'Poverty weighs on me worse than illness… For example, take this… It's the time to sow oats, and how is one to sow it if one has no seed?'

Marfa Petrovna is so moved by Zamuhrishen's gratitude that she offers to buy his seed for him; then he asks for a cow, and she promises him that too.

She notices that a little packet of red paper falls from his pocket as he speaks. After he has gone, she examines it, and finds that it contains the very pilules that she has prescribed for him. He has taken none of them, and a doubt begins to enter her mind. This doubt is confirmed when all the patients who follow him praise her curative skill extravagantly—and then ask for economic assistance.

Chekhov draws a short moral: 'The deceitfulness of Man!' Yet in the case of my mother... well, reality is a complex thing.

An inconvenient truth

Christa Wolf was the most famous East German writer, at least in the west. Her reputation suffered somewhat after the Berlin Wall came down from the revelation that she had informed for the Stasi, though only for a short time when she was young. She was widely regarded as an equivocal dissident, half-darling, half-opponent of the regime. One can't help thinking of the position of medical directors of NHS trusts.

Medicine has long been an interest of Christa Wolf's. The heroine of her most famous book, *The Quest for Christa T*, dies from leukaemia. In 1984 Wolf wrote an essay entitled 'Illness and Love Deprivation: Questions for Psychosomatic Medicine.' And in 1991 she gave a lecture to the German Cancer Society entitled Cancer and Society, in which she wondered whether there was a cancer personality that, because it was inhibited by its social upbringing from expressing aggression outwardly, turned its aggression inwards in the form of cancer. She quoted the Swiss author Fritz Zorn, who, like many a memoirist of cancer (or other fatal disease) from the privileged sector of society whom I have read, asked the question when he contracted the disease, 'Why me?' His answer was as follows:

The harm that is caused by faulty upbringing can be so great that in its most extreme forms it can manifest itself as a neurotically determined illness, such as cancer, as now seems to be the case with me.

This is what one might call the Rousseau theory of cancer: that in a virtuous state of nature, man would never get it. This raises the question of what man would die from in such a state (assuming he would not be immortal)—that is, if his upbringing were of a perfection of which Rousseau and Wolf might approve. The answer seems to be that he wouldn't live long enough to get cancer.

Wolf wonders whether there 'is a connection between the widespread inability to handle the truth of a serious illness and our deeply ingrained habit of deceiving ourselves, and letting ourselves be deceived, about the role we are playing and the society we live in?' Here one cannot help but remember T S Eliot's famous line, that humankind cannot bear very much reality.

Wolf says that 'many doctors who avoid the truth when dealing with patients are behaving normally, complying with the norms, conforming to their society'—which, of course, she feels, is all wrong. She seems to be an ally of Mr Grandgrind on this question: facts, and facts alone, are what is needed in life.

I think things are rather more complex, which is no doubt why mistakes are so often made. Where there is a need for judgment, there is always the possibility of error. I remember that when my mother had cancer, she demanded that after her operation she should be told everything. In fact, she had a poor prognosis (the likelihood of recurrence and death within a year was great) and the surgeon, sizing her up, advised against a full disclosure of the facts. She lived another 20 years, and I have little doubt that the surgeon was absolutely right and humane in his advice, which was to mislead, if not actually to deceive, her: or, in Christa Wolf's parlance, to behave normally.

Through the looking glass

Are there any depths of cruelty and absurdity to which bureaucracy cannot plunge? It seems unlikely that there are, an impression confirmed by reading Jean-Claude Dreyfus's short and laconic *Souvenirs lointains de Buchenwald et Dora, 1943-45*.

Dreyfus was a young doctor in Paris when the Second World War broke out. After the war he was to become a distinguished professor of biochemistry. During the first period of the occupation he continued to work in Parisian hospitals where, as a Jew, he experienced neither hostility nor sympathy.

Eventually it became too dangerous for him to remain in Paris, and he went to Lyon, where he assumed the identity of Raymond Leclerc, pretending to be a travelling salesman but actually working unpaid in the laboratory of Professor Gabriel Florence. When Florence was arrested as a leader of the Resistance, however, Dreyfus/Leclerc removed to Annecy, where he was himself arrested, not as a Jew but at random, as one of 40 people taken in reprisal for the killing of two German soldiers by the Resistance.

He went first to Buchenwald and then to Dora, where, to improve his living conditions and increase his chances of survival (in Buchenwald he had undergone several operations without anaesthesia on his leg for an abscess that left him weak and unable to do physical labour) he admitted to being a doctor.

Although people were dying all around from malnutrition and epidemic diseases, Dreyfus was obliged to undergo an academic examination by other doctor prisoners in the camp, to establish whether he really was a doctor. At the end of the examination he was granted entry to the camp's medical fraternity.

He was deputed to the ward for moribund patients with tuberculosis. Right up to the end of the war, into the last three or four months of it, these patients were examined radiographically and their sputum examined bacteriologically, though of course there was no treatment. When they died their names and numbers were entered punctiliously into a book for the purpose; once there was a crisis when Dreyfus mistakenly entered the wrong number of a deceased person in the book. He could have been relieved of his duty because (it was explained to him) terrible suffering might result if relatives were wrongly informed of a death. It didn't matter, of course, that no such information was ever given out, and that by then the allies were only a few miles to the east and the west and all communication with the outside world had ceased.

Dreyfus's daughter related that he never spoke of his experiences once he returned from Germany. His short memoirs were written at his family's request and not published until nine years after his death in 1995. The epigraph to the book is, 'To remain silent is forbidden, to speak impossible.'

My mother was a refugee from Nazi Germany, arriving in Britain in 1939. She never saw her parents again, who escaped later to Shanghai; she never spoke a single word about her life between 30 January 1933 and the battle of Britain.

After her death I found letters from her father, a doctor, written to her from Shanghai. In 1942 he wrote, 'It is a beautiful spring morning and the sun is shining brightly, but there is no sun bright enough to penetrate the dark clouds that are covering the whole earth.'

Three years later her sister, also in Shanghai, wrote to her to ask in which language she wanted their parents' tombs, English or German.

2. Makes Death an Evil

A puzzle

Every author, I suppose, is familiar with the experience of realising the mistakes he has made the very moment that what he has written has been committed irrevocably to print. And this was so with a book of mine published this year titled *The Policeman and the Brothel*. I had overlooked something that should have been obvious to me, at least as a possibility.

My wife, who is a doctor, was doing a locum on the island of Jersey and I went with her. Finding myself with nothing to do there for three or four months, I researched three murders that took place there between December 1845 and February 1846, the last of them of a policeman called Le Cronier, by a brothel-keeper called Madame Le Gendre, and wrote a book about them.

Among other things I discovered in the course of my researches was that about a half of all the newspaper proprietors or editors of provincial newspapers in Britain at the time were also vendors of patent medicines. This was a case of commercial synergy, since patent manufacturers were by far the largest advertisers in their newspapers. And half of the advertisements were for remedies for syphilis, *ergo*... well, I don't need to point out the moral.

One of the murders was by a man called Thomas Nicolle, the scion of a respectable family. Not sober, he went to a café in Saint Helier late at night and there had a quarrel with the owner over a bar tab for two bottles of champagne (six shillings). The owner threw him out, followed him, and knocked him down in the street. Nicolle went back to his lodgings, fetched a gun, returned to the café and shot at random through the shutters, killing a man called Simon Abraham who was having a late night game of cards there.

Nicolle was sentenced to death, but his advocate went to London to obtain a reprieve from the home secretary, who granted it on the grounds that Nicolle had in the past been mad. I quote now what I wrote about some of the evidence at his trial:

According to [his landlady], his behaviour appeared strange and completely inexplicable on a number of occasions. For example she had seen him beating the walls with his fists until they bled... One night he slept in a box in his room instead of on his bed. [She] had never seen him drunk, and said that he was known... as Mad Nicolle.

At the time of his madness he was learning his trade, which was that of—a hatter. Obviously, he was a mad hatter, but astonishingly and mortifyingly I missed this in my book. His symptoms, which fit no commonly seen pattern nowadays, were those of erethism caused by mercury poisoning. H A Waldron, in an article on the Mad Hatter in the *BMJ* in 1983, said the psychotic symptoms of erethism were excessive timidity, diffidence, increasing shyness, a desire to remain unobserved, and an explosive loss of temper when criticised.

The treatment in those days was plenty of fresh air. Nicolle's sentence was commuted to transportation for life to Van Diemen's Land, where presumably he did get plenty of fresh air. And it might have cured him, because he does not appear in the criminal records of Van Diemen's Land or New Zealand, where he died.

How could I possibly have overlooked so obvious a diagnosis? But of course kind readers will point out that I have overlooked something in this article too.

An empty stomach

No doubt it is unusual for the founders of great institutions of learning to be deliberately poisoned to death with strychnine, let alone at the second attempt, but such seems to have been the fate in 1905 of the immensely rich Jane Stanford, the joint founder of

Stanford University. First someone put strychnine in her mineral water in San Francisco, and then in her bicarbonate of soda in Honolulu, to which she had escaped to recover from the physical and emotional shock of having been poisoned.

The president of Stanford University at the time was a medical man, a keen eugenicist and ichthyologist, called David Starr Jordan, who was much in favour of compulsory sterilisation of so called unfit individuals. For some reason, perhaps never to be explained, he worked hard to cover up the fact that Stanford had been poisoned and was successful in his endeavours. He himself had a motive, namely that Stanford was about to dismiss him from his post; but, unlike Stanford's personal secretary, Bertha Berner, who was the only person present at both poisonings, he lacked the opportunity. Berner, by contrast, lacked a motive.

Jordan managed to divert public attention from the opinion of four doctors that Stanford had been poisoned by citing the opinion of a young doctor, Ernest Waterhouse, that she had died of heart disease, brought on or exacerbated by eating too much at a picnic (despite the fact that her stomach was empty at postmortem examination) and unaccustomed exercise (she had walked a short distance).

Jordan maintained that the strychnine that was found in Mrs Stanford's bicarbonate of soda had been put there after she died by her physician, Dr F H Humfris, to defend his diagnosis of strychnine poisoning. He also suggested that the analytical chemist who had found it (and found it also in her body), Dr Edmund Shorey, was in on the conspiracy. Although the coroner's jury found that Stanford had been murdered, the police dropped the case, and journalists eventually accepted that she had died from natural causes.

The fates of the principal doctors involved, Humfris and Waterhouse, diverged. Jordan claimed that the former (who was present at the death) was incompetent and unprofessional, while the latter was extremely knowledgeable. Humfris, an Englishman, returned to England, where he became a distinguished advocate of actinotherapy, which is the therapeutic application of light, writing textbooks on the subject that went through several editions (he used it as a prophylactic against congenital rickets, and it might have been partly due to him that I was put regularly under a sun lamp as a child). Waterhouse left Honolulu to become a rubber planter in Malaya and Sumatra, lost all his money, and died down and out, selling newspapers in the street in New York.

This story is wonderfully investigated in *The Mysterious Death of Jane Stanford*, by Robert W P Cutler, emeritus professor of neurology at Stanford. The book was published in 2003, a year before his own death from metastatic lung cancer. Cutler, who was an expert on Parkinson's disease and published a review of the diagnostic use of cerebrospinal fluid in the very year of his death, wrote it while more or less permanently on oxygen, a tribute, surely, to human courage.

Good old charity

What is the most characteristic British institution? The National Health Service, perhaps? No. It is the charity shop. In no country in the world are there so many charity shops as in Great Britain. Is it because the British are so charitable?

I leave it to others, more learned in political economy than I, to decide why we should have so many charity shops; suffice it to say that I rarely pass such a shop without glancing at the books for sale in them, for often, among the ranks of trashy paperback novels is one book worth having.

One day, for example, I went into a charity shop—one of many—in a dismal little town in Gloucestershire (also one of many) and found *Camps on Crime*, by the late Professor Francis E Camps, published in 1973.

It was a bargain, marked down (said the label) from £2 to £1. Were there people, I wondered, who would not buy it at the higher price, but would buy it at the lower? Anyway, I, if not the charity shop, was in luck.

A pencil drawing of Professor Camps adorned the cover: avuncular, smiling gently, drawing on his pipe—it once would have connoted mature wisdom, but would now connote a disregard of the safety of others.

Camps belonged to what might be called the heroic age of forensic pathology when (perhaps because crime itself was less widespread as a pastime) forensic pathologists like Sir Bernard Spilsbury and Sir Sydney Smith were popular heroes. Camps was in apostolic succession to them, as it were, and like them was universally regarded by the public as a final court of appeal in matters of forensic pathology.

Murders in those days seemed so much more interesting—refined is perhaps not the word I seek—than those in ours. They seemed somehow to be so much more characteristically British than they do now, taking place as they did in seedy boarding houses and along country lanes. Of course, George Orwell pointed out the decline of the English murder a long time ago.

I decided to buy the book when, quite apart from its reduced price, I noticed an essay in it entitled 'The Mummy of Rhyl.' The combination of ancient Egypt and North Wales was quite irresistible.

I am glad to say that something of the old boarding house culture, in places like Colwyn Bay, persists along the north coast of Wales. The mummy of Rhyl was found in 1960 in a cupboard at number 35 West Kimmel Street, whose owner had for many years 'taken in paying guests.' I think the atmosphere is extremely well conveyed by the following description:

As the body was adherent to a piece of linoleum which covered the cupboard floor boards, a garden spade was used to lever it on the linoleum out of the cupboard and the position of the linoleum in relation to it was noted before they were separated with some difficulty.

Camps in this case was acting for the defence, and it could not be proved that the mummy, a paying guest since 1940, had not died of natural causes. However, the landlady, a Mrs Harvey, pleaded guilty to obtaining £2 a week for 20 years from the Clerk to the Justices of Prestatyn (who paid the mummy's pension) by pretending that the mummy was alive.

Even benefit fraud in those days seemed somehow more characterful.

A life of crime

William Roughead (1870–1952) was the doyen of British crime writers and might even be said to have invented the genre. The style of his essays was admired by Henry James; he was a friend of Joseph Conrad; and he knew JB Priestley. He also helped a famous doctor-writer, Arthur Conan Doyle, in his long campaign to exonerate Oscar Slater, wrongly imprisoned for a murder that he did not commit.

Roughead edited *Burke and Hare*, in the Notable British Trials series, providing in his introduction an excellent summary of the history of that pair who killed to furnish anatomy teachers with specimens to dissect. Occasionally, some of the criminals of whom he wrote were doctors themselves, such as Dr Dionysius Wielobycki, whose tomb in an Edinburgh graveyard intrigued him as a child. He later wrote an essay, *Physic and Forgery*, about him.

Wielobycki (1813–82) was a Polish exile who studied medicine in Edinburgh and established a successful and lucrative homoeopathic practice there. However, he decided he would like a little extra money and forged a will in his own favour, supposedly written in an old woman's own hand. He was caught because although the old woman was all but illiterate, he wrote the will in the most arcane legal language, which immediately aroused suspicion of the canny lawyers who disputed its terms. He was found guilty and sentenced to 14 years' transportation 'beyond the seas,' but was released after five years' imprisonment in Wandsworth and Pentonville. He then married a Polish countess.

You can't write long about murder without mentioning doctors, and the famous forensic pathologists of his days bestride Roughead's pages: John Glaister, Sydney Smith, Bernard Spilsbury. In his essay *My First Murder* (and he is said to have attended every 'important' murder trial in Scotland for half a century, though this raises the intriguing question of what an 'unimportant' murder trial might be), he describes how in 1889 he played truant from the lawyer's office in which he was training to be a writer, that is to say a solicitor, to attend a trial for murder, and was thereafter addicted to attendance at such trials.

The case did not, as Sherlock Holmes might have said, present many difficulties. It was of a woman who accepted illegitimate babies for a small sum of money to pay for their keep and then killed them. At the trial three doctors gave evidence: Henry Littlejohn, later knighted when professor of forensic medicine in Edinburgh, Harvey Littlejohn, his son and also later professor of forensic medicine in Edinburgh, and Dr Joseph Bell, the prototype of Sherlock Holmes. Because of the condition of the dead babies, none of the doctors could swear to the cause of death, although the ligatures around their necks gave a clue.

I was reminded of my own first murder. A man had stabbed his wife and then put his head in the oven (in those days you could still gas yourself courtesy of the Gas Board). The defence counsel in his final address to the jury made much of the connection between the man's unhappy childhood and his decision to kill his wife.

'I should have thought,' the judge interrupted him, 'that the fact that his wife attacked him first was sufficient explanation.'

'Oh yes, milord, I was just coming to that,' said the defence counsel, but he had obviously forgotten it. I learnt that it isn't only doctors who can be incompetent.

The doctor writer's handbook

Every so often a junior doctor would come to me and confess that he or she wanted to write. This was not in itself absurd: the number of doctor writers is, after all, legion.

Junior doctors afflicted with literary ambition would ask my advice. I had only three pieces of advice to give: firstly, that they should continue in the hospital for a few more years, because human nature was concentrated and distilled there as if for the express purpose of training writers; secondly, that on no account should they consort with academics of the humanities departments of any university, for to do so was the primrose path to stylistic perdition; and finally, that they should read a great deal.

'Yes, but what?' they would ask.

'There are two books that you should study,' I would reply. 'The first is *A Companion to Murder* by E Spencer Shew, and the second is *A Second Companion to Murder* by E Spencer Shew, published in 1960 and 1961 respectively.'

This recommendation rather took my interlocutors by surprise—they had probably expected me to recommend Tolstoy or Shakespeare. But the study of the works of E Spencer Shew, who was for many years crime correspondent of the *Daily Express*, would be more immediately profitable, for it is a fact that, despite the lengthy subtitles of his books—A Dictionary of Death by Poison, Death by Shooting, Death by Suffocation and Drowning, Death by the Strangler's Hand, and A Dictionary of Death by the Knife, the Dagger, the Razor; Death by the Axe, the Chopper, the Chisel; Death by the Iron File, the Marline Spike; Death by the Hammer, the Poker, the Bottle; Death by the Jemmy, the Spanner, the Tyre Lever, the Iron Bar, the Starting Handle; Death by the Sandbag, the Sash Weight; Death by the Mallet, the Half-brick, the Stick, the Stone; Death by the Fire Tongs, the Butt End of a Revolver; Death by the Metal Chair, etc—Shew was a master of concision, who could convey atmosphere and character in a few exquisitely chosen words.

Open the book anywhere and you will find little gems of concision (which is next to godliness) in the first two or three lines of an entry. Here is Dr Crippen: 'Crippen, Hawley Harvey, with his bulbous eyes, straggling moustache, choker collar, mild manners, indestructible air of respectability, florid wife, and mouse-like mistress, is the central figure of the one indisputable murder 'classic' of the twentieth century.'

There is much of medical interest in these two volumes, so that even if our literary junior doctors do not succeed in their ambitions they will not entirely have lost their time in reading them. The murderous doctor is there, in the person of Dr Buck Ruxton who, in his own words, could live neither with his wife nor without her but decided that the latter was the preferable alternative; so is the great forensic pathologist Sir Bernard Spilsbury; and also an unfortunate succession of GPs, whose erroneous diagnoses of epilepsy so assisted the Brides in the Bath murderer, George Joseph Smith, 'murderer, bigamist, swindler, performer on the harmonium.' Never did misdiagnosis have worse consequences.

It is not only stylistic concision that one learns from E Spencer Shew but the useful lesson that, in the way of human wickedness, there is no new thing under the sun. Nurse Waddingham, for example, poisoned the more demanding clients of her nursing home with morphine. A complete education, in fact.

Lethal lies

Sometimes I wake in a sweat having dreamt that my school exam papers have been marked again, and it has been determined that I failed. As a result, my entry to medical school was invalid and the rest of my subsequent career fraudulent. I shall have to begin my life all over again.

This is a common dream, of course, though I am not sure whether in my case it signifies general anxiety or is a manifestation of what the great political print artist James Gillray called 'the horrors of digestion.' He who eats late at night must expect to fail his exams repeatedly.

One of the most remarkable books that I have read in recent years is *The Adversary* by Emmanuel Carrère. It recounts the life of Jean-Claude Romand, a medical student at Lyon who, having failed to turn up for his second year exams, lied to his parents that he had passed them.

He maintained the lie for the next 20 years, passing himself off after his equally fictitious qualification as a doctor working for the World Health Organization in Geneva. He lived with his wife, whom he managed to deceive just as he deceived everyone else, on the French side of the border, going off every day to 'work,' that is, to say spending time in the public parts of the WHO building, or in cafes and parks, reading books and newspapers. Sometimes he would claim to have gone to conferences abroad, and would return with jet lag and appropriate presents for the children, but would have spent the time in local hotels. There he would read up on information about the country he was supposed to have visited.

He maintained his expensive lifestyle, commensurate with a WHO salary, by using the savings of his parents and others, acting as an intermediary for lucrative investments in Switzerland.

He kept the lies going for many years but when exposure became inevitable he killed his parents, his wife, and his two children, and then burnt his house down, having taken barbiturates, in an attempt at suicide. He was rescued, however, and survived.

The author manages the difficult trick of evoking compassion for 'Dr' Romand, while not minimising his crime in any way. What drove Jean-Claude Romand to such a pass? I think it was the ordinary sin of pride, and because we all commit that sin very often we can enter imaginatively into his predicament.

Once when I was in Argentina a man who had been a famous neurologist was exposed as a fraud, as having no medical qualification whatsoever. He really did attend international conferences, where he would always begin his presentations on abstruse subjects with words to the effect that 'You don't have to be a doctor to be a neurologist.' Everyone laughed: how he must have loved to hear scores or hundreds of properly qualified people made a fool of in this way!

After reading Carrère, my dream recurred several times, and for a short time I found myself in a panic anxiously asking, to quote a famous medical student and poet, 'Do I wake or sleep?'

A box of tricks

Transcripts of trials almost always make good reading, but perhaps that is because only those of interesting trials are ever published. Their literary quality is high, but they also have the advantage of an inherently dramatic structure with a built-in climax. The longueurs of trials in real life are, of course, edited out.

The transcript of one trial in Manchester was published in 1933 by the accused, under the title 'The Black Box Trial.' It was reprinted five years later.

Charles Clement Abbott was accused of manslaughter. For many years he had practised as 'a physio-medicalist' practitioner. He was a former miner who had suffered from tuberculosis and, having been given up as a hopeless case, went to a herbalist who cured him. He then took up herbalism himself.

He also believed in Dr Albert Abrams's 'Electronic Reactions of

Abrams.' Abrams (1863-1924) was an American quack who believed that the tissues and bodily fluids of diseased persons gave off special electronic vibrations according to the disease and that these could be detected when a healthy subject, put in contact with the bodily fluid by means of a wire and placed in a black wire box to prevent the influence of extraneous radiations, had a glass rod passed over his abdomen. The diagnosis was made according to the part of the abdominal wall that experienced tension when the glass rod passed over it.

This astonishing nonsense was taken sufficiently seriously to be investigated by the American Medical Association and by a committee under the chairmanship of Sir Thomas (later Lord) Horder. The writers Arthur Conan Doyle and Upton Sinclair believed in Abrams's method, as did many others: Abrams left an immense fortune when he died in the month and year that he had predicted for himself.

The case over which Abbott found himself arraigned was that of a young boy with meningitis. Abbott did not believe in the germ theory of disease, or in the serum therapy that had reduced the death rate from meningococcal meningitis from 80% in 1910 to roughly 20% by 1930, though serum therapy did not alter the universally fatal prognosis from pneumococcal meningitis. The effect on haemophilus meningitis was slight, reducing the death rate to 85%.

Abbott did not send the boy to hospital for a lumbar puncture because he believed lumbar puncture to be dangerous. The boy died, and Abbott was charged with manslaughter, being called by the prosecutor 'an absolutely ignorant and impudent impostor.'

Much of the evidence called on both sides was beside the point, though very entertaining to read. His defence lawyer, Mr E G Hemmerde KC, mentioned that George Bernard Shaw, then at the height of his fame, agreed with many of Abbott's views, but Shaw was in many respects the archetype of the absolutely ignorant and impudent impostor. Mr Hemmerde also compared Abbott with Semmelweis, which was intellectually unscrupulous: if scientific genius is sometimes persecuted, being persecuted is not necessarily a sign of scientific genius.

Abbott could not have been found guilty of manslaughter because it could not possibly be proved beyond reasonable doubt that the boy would have survived had he been sent to hospital and received the then orthodox treatment. He subsequently published the transcript of the trial, the action not of an impostor, but of a sincerely deluded man—a far more dangerous type.

3. Sanity

Doctors are said to make very bad patients. Two stories are known to me in which psychiatrists become inmates of their own asylum. The first, 'Ward 6', a story by the writer and doctor Anton Chekhov (1860-1904), is very well known. The second, by the greatest Brazilian writer, Machado de Assis (1839-1908), was written a few years before *Ward 6* and is less well known in the English speaking world. It is the novella *O Alienista*, *The Alienist* or (as it is usually translated) *The Psychiatrist*.

A doctor, Simon Bacamarte, returns to Brazil after his studies in Coimbra and Padua and settles in the small town of Itaguai. With a deep passion for science and a complete faith in its powers of redemption, he wants to penetrate the secrets of madness and persuades the municipal council to open an asylum under his direction, called the Green House, so that he can unravel those secrets.

What follows reads like a prescient satire on the *Diagnostic and Statistical Manual* of the American Psychiatric Association. The first thing for Dr Bacamarte to do is to classify the mad, in the style of the DSM: 'first two great classes, then sub-classes, then sub-sub-classes into which cases, ever more aberrant, were increasingly more difficult to place.'

Unsurprisingly, more and more of the people of Itaguai are admitted by force into the Green House until four fifths of the entire population of the town are lodged there, including Dr Bacamarte's own wife, who he realises is mad when she cannot decide whether to wear her sapphire or her garnet necklace to a forthcoming ball and gets up in the middle of the night to try them on in front of the mirror.

The increasing number of people admitted to the Green House eventually causes a revolt, in the course of which 11 people are killed. This gives Dr Bacamarte pause: perhaps his theory has been wrong all along. Perhaps it is the sane, those with perfect mental equilibrium, the small minority, who should be admitted to the asylum. Dr Bacamarte gets the municipal council to grant him powers to admit all the well balanced people (excluding members of the council, of course) to the asylum.

There he classifies them as he once classified the mad: the modest, the loyal, the wise, the patient, and so on. He devises a scientific method of disequilibriating them—for example, he gives the modest a tail coat, a wig, or a cane, and they at once become full of themselves. Those refractory to the treatment are given diamonds to wear or an official decoration.

Before long, everyone is 'cured' of being normal, and Dr Bacamarte discharges them from the asylum. But he is still an enthusiast to know more, and in the end he admits himself to the asylum, where he dies 17 months later. The rumour then spreads that there had never been a madman in Itaguai other than Dr Bacamarte himself. 'Be that as it may,' the story ends, 'his funeral was conducted with great pomp and rare solemnity.'

Surely anyone who has worked (at least as a doctor) in the NHS cannot but have wondered who are the mad and who the sane?

The meaning of everything

Sixteen years before Karl Jaspers described primary delusions in his textbook, *General Psychopathology*, first published in 1913, Checkov's 'Ward No 6' gave an account of such a delusion. In this story, a provincial doctor, Andrei Yefimitch Ragin, is himself ultimately admitted to the ward for lunatics whom he has long neglected and whose suffering he has equally long ignored.

One of the patients in ward 6 is Ivan Dmitritch Gromov. The Gromov family fortunes had begun to decline when his brother died of consumption; his father, an official, is then arrested for misappropriation of funds and dies of typhoid in the prison hospital. Young

Ivan Dmitritch is obliged to leave the university and take a job, ending up as a court usher.

Somewhat awkward in human company, he was what one might call a morbid or pathological reader, using the printed word as a substitute for real life, 'devouring the pages without giving himself time to digest what he read' and falling upon 'anything that came into his hands with equal avidity, even last year's newspapers and calendars.'

Then one morning:

In one of the side-streets he was met by two convicts in fetters and four soldiers with rifles in charge of them. Ivan Dmitritch had very often met convicts before... but now this meeting made a peculiar, strange impression on him. It suddenly seemed to him for some reason that he, too, might be put into fetters and led through the mud to prison like that.

From then on, Ivan Dmitritch interprets everything differently. '[O]n the way home he met near the post office a police superintendent of his acquaintance, who greeted him and walked a few paces along the street with him, and for some reason this seemed to him suspicious.'

He had not done anything wrong, yet thought he might soon become the victim of injustice because:

People who have an official, professional relation to other men's sufferings— for instance, judges, police officers, doctors—in course of time, through habit, grow so callous that they cannot, even if they wish it, take any but a formal attitude to their clients; in this respect they are not different from the peasant who slaughters sheep and calves in the back-yard, and does not notice the blood.

Chekhov captures here the preservation, even the sharpening, of the paranoid person's intellect and powers of reflection. Every small event is infused with sinister meaning: 'A policeman walking slowly passed by the windows: that was not for nothing. Here were two men standing still and silent near the house. Why were they silent?' Eventually, Ivan Dmitritch flees the house in the belief that the men who have come to repair the stove are policemen, and he is admitted to ward 6.

Jaspers, who was both psychiatrist and philosopher, gives examples of delusional mood in his *General Psychopathology*: 'Suddenly things seem to mean something quite different. The patient sees people in uniform in the street; they are Spanish soldiers. A patient noticed the waiter in the coffee-house; he skipped past him so quickly and uncannily. A passer-by gave such a penetrating glance, he could be a detective.' Jaspers made no mention of Ivan Dmitritch, however: surely a suspicious circumstance? What can it mean?

The invisible enemy

Guy de Maupassant (1850-93) wrote two versions of one of his best known stories, 'Le Horla'. In the first version, published in 1886, Dr Marrande, 'the greatest and most famous alienist,' invites three of his medical colleagues and four non-medical scientists to listen to one of his patients in his asylum, 'the most bizarre and disturbing case that I have ever known.'

It seems to us odd that the doctor should have arranged the evening, and invited laymen, almost as if to an entertainment. But Maupassant himself had attended the lectures and demonstrations of Charcot at La Salpêtrière, complete with clinical demonstrations of patients. Clearly the division between the medical and literary world was more permeable than it is now, and medical ethics a little looser. Of course, Maupassant was soon to become the patient of 'the greatest and most famous alienist' of his day, Dr Blanche, in whose asylum he stayed from January 1892 until his death from general paralysis of the insane in July 1893.

In the first version of 'Le Horla', the patient narrates his story to Dr Marrande's friends; in the second we read the diary of the nameless protagonist, who in both versions is struck by a strange ailment, the precise nature of which we, the readers, are never vouchsafed. Is it real or is it the product of madness? It comes on after the protagonist sees a Brazilian ship sail by; only later do we learn that there has been a mass outbreak of precisely the same ailment in Brazil—a true epidemic.

The Horla, the protagonist's neologism that is suggestive of the *au dela* (the other side), is a being that haunts and terrifies him, who is invisible to his senses but capable of producing effects in the physical world. The Horla is a bit like a poltergeist; the protagonist notices, for example, that it drinks his water at night when he is asleep. He thinks at first that he might have drunk the water himself while sleepwalking, so he locks the doors of his room before he goes to bed, covers his glass with a white cloth, and covers his hands with graphite. In the morning, the cloth has been moved but there is no graphite on it; it is the Horla who has drunk the water.

Maupassant makes a surprising reference in the second version to Paul Broca, of Broca's area (in the brain relating to speech), whose work he had read. Wondering whether he is mad, the protagonist writes that he could be suffering from a lesion such as that the physiologists of the day are trying to define and locate.

The protagonist experiences something like the passivity phenomena of schizophrenia: 'Someone possesses my soul and rules it! Someone orders all my acts, all my movements, all my thoughts. I am no longer anything in myself, nothing but a terrified spectator and slave of all that I do.'

The someone who possesses him is a superior being brought about by evolution (Maupassant had also read Darwin): 'A new being! Why not? It must surely come. Why should we be the last? The new being will enslave man as man has enslaved the animals.' Is it not ironic to think of the brain of the author of this story being eaten away by an enemy that was invisible to him?

The value of pulp fiction

There is more to great literature than good writing, of course, for even the most arrant nonsense can be well written. And it is my impression that the pulp writers of yesteryear were better stylists than the pulp writers of today.

Algernon Blackwood, for example, who lived from 1869 to 1951, was a fine stylist whose prose even contained subtle psychological and social observations. His plots are mainly absurd, but his urbanity is pleasurable. For example, *The Wings of Horus*, in which a man of overheated imagination believes himself possessed by the old Egyptian god, takes place before the First World War in an Egyptian hotel to which rich invalids have been sent by their doctors to recover. Blackwood writes, 'Excess and bed were their routine. They lived, but none of them got better.' That is very good.

Similarly, in *The Doll*, Madame Jodzka, the Polish governess, is horrified to see her charge's ugly little doll come alive. 'Making no audible sound, she screamed in her mind.' That, too, is very good.

One of Blackwood's heroes is John Silence, 'rich by accident and by choice a doctor.' He specialises in patients with metaphysical problems, or tangles with the supernatural, and naturally enough his practice attracts the occasional lunatic. For this Dr Silence is well prepared, for he has two waiting rooms:

One, intended for persons who imagined they needed spiritual assistance, when really they were only candidates for the asylum, had padded walls, and was well-supplied with various concealed contrivances by means of which sudden violence could be met and instantly overcome.

The other waiting room, for people with genuine metaphysical illnesses (such as Racine Mudge, son of a Frenchwoman from Bordeaux and a British grocer, who had a tendency to disappear into Higher Space, especially whenever he heard music by Wagner) was painted a soothing deep green, 'calculated to induce calmness and repose of mind.' Dr Silence chose his colour wisely: green is indeed the colour of anxiolysis (a conscious state of sedation).

The chairs in the waiting room were fixed to the floor, for Dr Silence had observed that when people were agitated they tended not only to shift in their chairs but to shift their chairs themselves, and this set up a kind of vicious circle: the more they moved, the more agitated they became. A fixed chair maketh a calm patient.

It so happens that in several of the prisons I have visited, particularly those that were privately run, the chairs in the interview rooms were fixed to the floor—though more, I suspect, to preserve property and prevent the physical expression of agitation than to prevent its development in the first place.

Just in case the wise provisions of green walls and immobile chairs failed completely to calm the nerves of the patients, Dr Silence had a button he could press that released a narcotic gas, 'swiftly effective but harmless,' into the room. I am not sure whether Dr Silence had a gas mask to avoid himself the soporific effects of the gas.

It will be seen from this brief conspectus of Blackwood's work that the reading of well selected pulp fiction is not a complete waste of time and may be indulged in without a sense of guilt. In fact, it can even be recommended for those in need of suggestions for improvements to the service.

The dangers of drinking green tea

The name Le Fanu is not unknown to medicine in this country. There is, for example, the medical correspondent of one of our major newspapers, and W R LeFanu, who was the librarian of the Royal College of Surgeons between 1929 and 1968. A man of immense erudition, which puts one's own ignorance to shame, he oversaw the removal of the library during the Second World War to Shropshire, saving it from the destruction that the college itself suffered during the Blitz. A bibliographer of distinction, especially in the field of Jennerian studies, he published a bibliography of Nehemiah Grew at the age of 86, in 1990.

Sheridan Le Fanu, the Irish writer of ghost stories, was an ancestor of his. Doctors featured very often in Le Fanu's stories; one book, *In a Glass Darkly*, published in 1872, is a series of the cases of one Dr Hesselius, a German specialist in 'metaphysical medicine.'

In the first and most famous of these stories, 'Green Tea', Dr Hesselius is consulted by the Reverend Mr Jennings, a clergyman in easy circumstances who, alas, is haunted. Already interested in the supernatural—books about which he stays up all night studying while drinking green tea—he one day sees two red eyes staring at him on an omnibus, which he then makes out to belong to a spectral monkey through which his umbrella can pass without meeting any resistance. The monkey stays with him for the rest of his days and grows ever more intrusive, jumping on to the Bible when he tries to read from it in church, so that he is unable to continue the service, then uttering terrible blasphemies whenever the Reverend Jennings tries to pray, and finally issuing him with commands, including that to commit suicide. Eventually, he does kill himself, by cutting his throat.

Dr Hesselius's diagnosis of the Reverend Jennings's distemper is cautious. It is one of Le Fanu's themes that we can never fully or definitively interpret events, and Dr Hesselius is of like opinion. In this case, he goes in for what one might call agnostic multifactorialism. First was 'the habitual use of such agents as green tea,' which disturb the equilibrium of the cerebral fluids. Interestingly, a National Institute of Health website informs us that when more than 8 to 10 cups of green tea per day are drunk, 'symptoms of anxiety, delirium, agitation and psychosis may occur.' Nor is stopping the tea necessarily instantly beneficial in those with 'affective disorder or schizoaffective disorder,' in whom withdrawal from the caffeine can cause 'confusion, disorientation, excitement, restlessness, violent behaviour, or mania.'

In Dr Hesselius's opinion, one of the effects of the tea is to influence the brain so that 'disembodied spirits may operate in communication more effectually.' He thus makes it unclear as to whether he believes the black monkey with red eyes is a hallucination pure and simple, or an actually existing entity.

But Dr Hesselius doesn't blame the tea alone. '[Jennings'] case was in the distinctive manner a complication, and the complaint under which he really succumbed, was hereditary suicidal mania.' So he was predisposed to kill himself, green tea and black monkey, or no green tea and black monkey.

As to therapy, Dr Hesselius says that iced eau de cologne applied to the forehead would inevitably have worked if applied long enough.

What rubbish! Everyone knows that what the Reverend Jennings needed was an SSRI (selective serotonin reuptake inhibitor), because serotonin is the key to all human happiness and misery, and indeed to all behaviour whatsoever.

The casualties of Waugh

My father was not very good at telling jokes. If something was a fact he couldn't leave it out, and over-inclusiveness is not an aid to mirth.

Still, he had a repertoire of old favourites, and one of them, which he told many times, concerned what in those days was still popularly known as the loony bin.

An inmate showed the chairman of the board of visitors around the establishment, and did so with such lucidity that the chairman asked him why he was an inmate at all. He replied that he didn't know, and asked the chairman to help him secure his release. The chairman promised to do so.

Just as he was leaving the asylum, the chairman felt a blow with a brick on the back of his head.

'Don't forget now,' said the inmate, waving to him.

This joke is, in essence, identical to the plot of Evelyn Waugh's short story *Mr Loveday's Little Outing*. Lord Moping is committed to the County Asylum for Mental Defectives (a term still widely in use during my childhood, although educationally subnormal was taking over) when he tries to hang himself during his wife's annual garden party. Lady Moping refuses to countenance a more expensive establishment because she has been so humiliated by his social faux pas; but the richer lunatics have a wing of their own in the asylum, where they are allowed to dress as they please and to have a dinner party every year on the anniversary of their committal.

Mr Loveday, another long term inmate, acts as Lord Moping's amanuensis during his residence in the asylum. Lord Moping is forever dictating memoranda to the great ones of the earth on such subjects as the fate of major rivers, and his daughter, Angela, is so impressed on a visit to her father by the efficiency of Mr Loveday, who tells her that many years ago he made the slight mistake of knocking a girl off her bicycle and then strangling her, that she vows to secure his release. Mr Loveday tells her that he has only one small ambition, but does not want to say what it is.

This she does, and a meeting is held in the asylum to send Mr Loveday off to his freedom. The doctor assures him that he is so highly esteemed by both staff and patients that there will always be a place for him if he does not like life outside.

Mr Loveday is back within two hours; and all too predictably, he has knocked a young woman off her bicycle and strangled her. He announces with the greatest pleasure that now he will never be released from the asylum again. He had never really wanted to go in the first place.

What exactly is Waugh satirising in his story? Not least, surely, the do-gooding propensities of the well-placed, who are inclined to take up causes whimsically as a means to mere self gratification, without much thought for the possible consequences.

Of course, these days Mr Loveday wouldn't have been released without a proper risk assessment and follow up arrangements. I'm not sure that would have preserved the young woman on the bicycle, however.

4. Intoxication

Malcolm Lowry's dry period

As every doctor knows, it is one thing to dry out an alcoholic and quite another to get him to stop drinking afterwards. Maybe it isn't even the doctor's role to do so: after all, are they their patients' keepers?

In any case, some alcoholics have so destroyed their lives, and for so long, that they might as well go on. What will they do if they give up drinking? Malcolm Lowry (1909-57), author of *Under the Volcano*, seemed not to fall into this lamentable category. Strikingly good looking, he was only 47 when he died, a talented and famous author, and might have written many more books.

On the other hand, heavy drinking seems to have been so large a part of his experience of life that he had almost nothing else to write about. He started drinking when he was 14, and never gave up for long. He died having taken too many sleeping pills as well as drink, though whether deliberately or by accident no one knows for certain.

His novella, *Lunar Caustic*, was first published posthumously in 1963, but he had started writing it in 1937. It recounts his time in Bellevue Hospital in New York, to which he was admitted in 1936, probably in a state of delirium tremens. 'Lunar caustic' is another name for silver nitrate used as a cautery or antiseptic; I remember using it early in my career in an attempt to stop persistent nosebleed. Was it his memory of his time in hospital or his alcoholism that he was trying to cauterise with it?

Lowry admitted himself to Bellevue voluntarily, his ward companions being a Jewish refugee and an innocent seeming adolescent boy who had cut the throat of a little girl with a broken bottle. 'Gee, it was only a little scratch,' he said when asked why he had done it. No reason is forthcoming. I have known more than a few patients who broke their lover's jaw or skull with 'just a slap.'

The conditions in Bellevue are awful; it is a world of brutality, where the staff bark orders at the patients and therapy consists mainly of intermittent basket weaving. The doctor, Dr Claggart, recognises in Lowry an educated man, not frequently encountered among the patients, and singles him out for philosophical conversation.

According to Lowry, there is little difference between the staff and the patients. It is the world that is mad, not the lunatic. He says to the doctor: 'You're as resigned as your wretched patients, and you not only stand for it, but persistently your technique is to try and adjust them back to the system—just as you might imagine wounded soldiers being patched up to be sent back to fight by surgeons who had been smashed up themselves.'

This is R D Laing *avant la lettre*: the madman is simply one who has seen clearer and further than the so called sane.

Lowry is discharged from Bellevue, not because he is deemed fit to go but because, as a foreigner, he is not entitled to public assistance. Not that it makes any difference, for within minutes he is back to drinking, never having resolved to stop: 'He was elated now, feeling the fire of the whisky.'

Coleridge's claret

As is well known, Samuel Taylor Coleridge was an opium addict. He took opium in the form of laudanum, that is to say tincture of opium in alcohol, which he drank by the pint. In addition, he was no mean bibber of claret; not a 21-unit-a-week man (or whatever the latest safe level of consumption is), but more like an all-you-can-drink man.

Several witnesses testified to his morning shakes and sweats, which improved after his first laudanum of the day, and in general this has been taken as evidence of his addiction to opium. However, it seems to me more likely that he was suffering from the withdrawal effects of alcohol. The trouble for literary types is that alcohol is a good deal less romantic than opium, and Coleridge was nothing if not Romantic.

His poem 'The Pains of Sleep' has often been taken also as a description of what were called 'opium dreams.' I think, however, that Coleridge's unpleasant dreams were more likely to have been the consequence of alcoholic excess than of his consumption of opium. Is there any of us who has not tossed and turned after drinking too much, and dreamed vividly and disturbingly? I don't want to be too autobiographical, but I certainly have. Coleridge drank so much, indeed, that he might well have had the DT's (delirium tremens).

In his little preface to the poem 'Kubla Khan: Or, a Vision in a Dream,' Coleridge tells us that in 1797,

> *... the Author, then in ill health, had retired to a lonely farm between Porlock and Linton... In consequence of a slight indisposition, an anodyne [laudanum] had been prescribed, from the effects of which he fell asleep in his chair at the moment he was reading this sentence... 'Here the Khan Kubla commanded a palace to be built, and a stately garden thereunto... And thus ten miles of fertile ground were inclosed within a wall.'*

Coleridge says he composed the poem in his sleep, committing it to paper when he woke. From thence came the famous lines, bubbling up from his subconscious genius: 'In Xanadu did Kubla Khan/A stately pleasure dome decree.../So twice five miles of fertile ground/With walls and towers were girdled round.'

Unfortunately, a man from Porlock called on business and interrupted the transcription of the lines, which Coleridge then forgot, which explains (according to Coleridge) why the poem was never completed. Actually, throughout his life Coleridge failed to complete quite a lot, even without men from Porlock to interrupt him.

But equally unfortunately, and brilliant as he was, Coleridge was never very wedded to the truth, and the story about the man from Porlock has been shown to be not merely untrue but a lie. The chief object of Coleridge's romanticism was always himself.

In 'The Pains of Sleep,' Coleridge tells us, with his usual liberal use of exclamation marks that are supposed to tell us how deeply he felt and suffered, that he was prey to: 'Fantastic passions! maddening brawl!/And shame and terror over all!'

Towards the end of the poem, Coleridge asks why he should have suffered such horrible visions and emotions, more appropriate to evil men: 'Such griefs with such men well agree,/But wherefore, wherefore, fall on me?'

I think the answer is obvious: too much claret, dear STC, too much claret.

Mind the quality smoking

I was told by those who knew the French well (because they are French themselves) that no one would obey the law that prohibited smoking in cafes and restaurants: that they would go down fighting to preserve the right to their immemorial fug. But when I went to Paris soon after the law came into force, I found that the French had obeyed the law, if not quite as lambs to the slaughter, then at least as hypochondriacs to the panacea.

While in Paris I bought a book by the great Sinologue and literary critic Simon Leys. He is a stylist both in English and French; what is even more impressive and unusual is that he puts his style to the service of truth and profundity. His books during the Cultural Revolution and its western apologists were at once so erudite and so witty (though the subject was no laughing matter). They were clear sighted at a time when many intellectuals had blinded themselves.

His book *The Happiness of Little Fish* is a collection of his short but concentrated and penetrating literary commentaries, written from Australia, where he died. Several times he brings up our obsession with the evils of smoking. For example, he quotes an opinion of tobacco that it is one of the most dangerous of poisons (a common enough view) and only afterwards lets us know the source of this opinion: Adolf Hitler. He is not trying to imply, of course, that smoking is good for the health; only that enthusiasm for the anti-smoking cause is not necessarily a sign of virtue and goodness of heart.

In his little essay, 'Cigarettes are divine' (the title of a book that

Leys says he has bought but not yet read, for fear that it says exactly what he would say in a book on that subject that he has long dreamed of writing), he tells us that Mozart, in one of his letters, said that he thought of death every day, and that this thought of mortality was the inspiration of all his musical creation. And Leys says that this (quite apart from his genius) explains the inexhaustible joy of his art.

He continues:

> *I do not want to claim that the inspiration we may derive from the funereal warnings by various health organisations and right-thinking people will turn all smokers into Mozart, but certainly strident reminders paradoxically come to adorn the use of tobacco with a new seductiveness, if not with a metaphysical significance. Each time I see one of those menacing slogans on a packet of cigarettes, I am seriously tempted to resume smoking.*

Leys is here raising the question, in the most delicate possible way, of what life is for: a question that we, as doctors, are professionally prohibited (quite rightly) from asking, let alone answering. Where human life is concerned, we have no choice but to take the purely quantitative view: the more of it for each individual the better. For us, therefore, Hitler's life was twice as successful as Schubert's, because he lived twice as long.

Tolstoy contra mundum

The first campaigner against passive smoking was probably the greatest novelist the world has ever known, Leo Tolstoy. In his essay 'Why do Men Stupefy Themselves?'—published in 1890 as an introduction to a book by his medical brother in law, Dr S P Alexeyev, with the title *Drunkenness* (he was against it)—Tolstoy wrote:

> *Everyone of average education considers it inadmissible, ill bred, and inhumane to infringe the peace, comfort, and yet more the health of others for his own pleasure. But out of a thousand smokers not one will shrink from producing unwholesome smoke in a room where the air is breathed by non-smoking women and children.*

Bravo for Tolstoy, you might say. And with his usual grasp of psychology he understands that the polite question 'Do you mind if I smoke?' is not a genuine request for information on the acceptability of smoking to a non-smoker, any more than the question from a nurse to patient 'What would you like to be called' is neutral as to whether first name or surname is proffered. For 'Do you mind if I smoke?' almost invariably calls forth the answer 'Not at all,' even when the non-smoker detests smoking and all its works; just as the nurse's question is answered 'Bill' rather than 'Professor Smith,' even if this is what he wants to be called.

The problem with the essay is that Tolstoy is mad, in the loose sense of the term. He begins it with a very pertinent question that I am sure we all as doctors have often asked—about our patients, of course, not about ourselves: 'What is the explanation of the fact that people use things that stupefy them—vodka, wine, beer, hashish, opium, tobacco, and other things less common: ether, morphia, fly-agaric, etc?'

The answer for Tolstoy is crystal clear, for once he starts thinking about anything, doubt and qualification are removed from his mind (Chekhov once called him an ignoramus). It is that stupefaction is the means by which they quieten or suppress their conscience.

For Tolstoy there is no such thing as moderation. Nor is there any other possible reason for people to resort to things that stupefy them. And he has it in for smoking particularly, not on health grounds but because it clouds consciousness and makes people do stupid or wicked things they wouldn't otherwise do. He says that all decisions taken while smoking are like decisions taken by a drunkard.

His prime example is a rather surprising one:

Without any need whatever, a company is formed, capital collected, men labour, make calculations, and draw plans; millions of working days and thousands of tons of iron are spent to build the Eiffel Tower; and millions of people consider it their duty to climb up it, stop awhile on it, and then climb down again.

And this, all because they smoke! In case the reader should still harbour any doubts about the evils of smoking, Tolstoy goes on to attribute European militarism to the fact that all Europe's leaders smoked and were therefore 'drunkards who never reach a state of sobriety.'

There is really only one possible explanation for how the world's greatest writer of his time could have come to write such terrible nonsense. He must have been drunk.

Ancient brain driers

We tend to forget what it is to be young and to wish to appear older than we are. Every time, therefore, that I pass the bus stop nearest my house and see a pale youth loitering there, lighting the cigarette by means of which he hopes to persuade the world that he is both tough and fully adult, I want to snatch the wretched thing from his grasp and upbraid him for his foolishness. I never do, of course.

Perhaps I should simply put into his hand Dr Tobias Venner's tract, first published in 1623 and then again in 1650 and 1660, entitled *A Brief and Accurate Treatise Concerning the Fume of Tobacco, Which very many, in these dayes, doe too too licentiously use.*

Venner (1577-1660) was the first doctor to extol at book length the medicinal value of the waters of Bath, where he practised for many years and in whose abbey he is buried. He was an early advocate of brushing the teeth to avoid decay and bad breath, warned against drinking waters that had passed through lead pipes ('troublesome to the stomack, and ponderous to all the bowels,' though 'these hurts are well removed in their boyling'); he believed strongly in bran for the prevention and treatment of constipation. So preoccupied was he, indeed, with diet as the means to health that an unfriendly memoirist said of him that his brains were in his bowels.

Dr Venner is not quite so vehement in his denunciation as James I of England, who ended his *Counterblaste to Tobacco* with the ringing words 'a custom loathsome to the eye, hateful to the nose, harmful to the brain, dangerous to the lungs, and in the black stinking fume thereof nearest resembling the horrible stygian smoke of the pit that is bottomless.'

Nevertheless Dr Venner is eloquent enough:

It drieth the braine, dimmeth the sight, vitiateth the smell, dulleth and dejecteth both the appetite and the stomack, destroyeth the concoction, disturbeth the humours and spirits, corrupteth the breath, induceth a trembling of the limbs, exsiccateth the wind-pipe, lungs and liver, annoyeth the milt, scorcheth the heart, and causeth the bloud to be adusted.

This is not all—though what else it does will not be easily understood by modern readers: 'Moreover, it eliquateth the pinguie substance of the kidnies and absumeth the geniture.' To exsiccate is to dry out; to adust is to scorch; to eliquate is to melt the more fusible substances of an alloy leaving solid the less fusible ones. The pinguie substance is fat. To absume is to waste away, and the geniture is the human seed (Venner is quoted in the *Oxford English Dictionary* in its definition of both exsiccate and geniture).

In summary, then, the fume 'overthroweth the spirits, perverteth the understanding, and confoundeth the sense with a sudden astonishment and stupidity of the whole body.'

How I long to go up to a pale smoking youth and say to him: 'Foolish boy! Cease this minute from exsiccating your windpipe! Do not eliquate your pinguie substance! Refrain from absuming your geniture!'

It wouldn't work, of course. The only way to make youngsters stop smoking is to make it compulsory. Then it would be as odious to them as Latin declensions.

Tobacco rage

One day a comprehensive history of opposition to tobacco will be written. In it, James I's famous *Counterblaste* will be given an honourable mention, with its denunciation of tobacco and 'the black stinking fumes thereof, nearest resembling the horrible Stygian smoke of the pit that is bottomless.'

Less prominent in the history, no doubt, will be Thomas Reynolds' *Anti-Tobaccoism: Three Hundred and Sixty-Five interviews with Smokers, Chewers and Snufftakers in a Series of Letters to John Lee, One of the Vice-Presidents of the British Anti-Tobacco Society*, published some time in the 1850s, with 'prefatory remarks' by Thomas Hodgkin, of Hodgkin's disease, who opined that reading these letters would be more profitable to most persons than reading a fashionable novel.

Thomas Reynolds, who died in 1875, had once been an enthusiastic smoker, but underwent a conversion experience. The titles of his letters have a charm of their own: for example, Letter XIX is headed 'Interview with a tobacconist, who had been a chewer of tobacco— A snuff-taking young surgeon—With three other snuff-taking surgeons.' (The young surgeon did not live long, which Reynolds attributed to his habit.) Letter XXXIX is headed,

A smoker's experience and report of misdoings by smoking Ministers [of religion]—A London warehouseman fearing to trust himself on Southwark Bridge—A snuff-taker shaking off his doctor—A snuffer deploring smoking—A smoking forsaker of the means of grace.

In what he called his 'walks of usefulness,' he would wander the streets of London and other cities expostulating with smokers, not all of whom by any means appreciated his efforts. His arguments were half religious, half medical. In Cambridge, where he attempted to hold a public meeting against smoking, there was a disturbance.

I thought it probable that among the University gentlemen I might meet with opposition, and that indeed I desired to induce, but when I arose to commence my lecture, I was greeted with crowing in imitation of cocks, which the gentlemen performed with considerable ability. They crowed well, but their taste was bad. Things went from bad to worse: Some arose on the forms smoking cigars, and with caps in hand, bowed gracefully to a company of ladies in the gallery, amongst whom they threw lighted fire-works, which caused them to shriek with terror.

The mayor arrived with 25 policemen, and one of the students asked the mayor whether he would like a cigar. Then there was a fight. Reynolds quotes the report the following day in the *Cambridge Independent Press*:

So soon as the lecturer commenced to dilate against the practice of smoking,

66

the University men began to smoke and shout, offering every obstacle to the lecturer, who, losing his presence of mind, expressed himself somewhat warmly, and a general disturbance ensued...

This suggests that Dickens' depiction of the meeting of the Brick Lane branch of the United Grand Junction Ebenezer Temperance Association, in which the drunken Reverend Mr Stiggins accuses the meeting in general, and Brother Tadger in particular, of being drunk, was mere reportage, not caricature.

However, we must all approve of the sixth principle of the British Anti-Tobacco Society: 'It is the imperative of every lover of mankind, to unite in suitable efforts to remove this rapidly increasing evil, by exhibiting its injurious effects on the health, its degrading consequences on the morals, and its enslaving power on the habits, of its deluded victims, and also, by seeking to deter others, especially the young, from acquiring this unnecessary, offensive and injurious practice.' Amen.

5. Addiction

Kipling's opium dreams

Rudyard Kipling (1865-1936) was familiar with dysentery, fever, and delirium. In his early years as a journalist in Lahore, he took a lot of opium to control his bowels; in his unfinished autobiography, *Something of Myself*, referring to that period of his life, he writes, 'a man can work with a temperature of 104, even though next day he has to ask the office who wrote the article.' He sometimes wrote while delirious.

It is not surprising, then, that opium dreams, and illusions and hallucinations, are important in his first works of fiction—for example in *The Phantom Rickshaw*. The very first of his fictional works, written and published when he was only 19, is 'The Gate of a Hundred Sorrows,' an account of an opium den in Lahore narrated by a Eurasian *habitué* of it. Very brief, it is an astonishingly assured piece of work.

The narrator, Gabral Misquitta, is in receipt of a legacy that yields sixty rupees a month, which he entrusts to the owner of the opium den known as the Gate of a Hundred Sorrows, an old Chinese man called Fung-Tching. In return Misquitta has unlimited access to opium, which he calls the Black Smoke. Under the influence of the drug, the black and red dragons 'and things' that adorned the pillows 'used to move about and fight.'

Misquitta's notion of happiness is that of many people today, and perhaps explains why they go in for intoxication of one kind or another:

Sometimes when I first came to the Gate, I used to feel sorry for it; but that's all over and done with a long time ago, and I draw my sixty rupees fresh and fresh every month, and am quite happy. Not DRUNK happy, you know, but always quiet and soothed and contented.

Misquitta pays the highest tribute an addict can pay his dealer: 'He must have made a good thing out of me, but he always gave me clean mats and pillows, and the best stuff you could get anywhere.'

Unfortunately, the halcyon days end: Fung-Tching dies and the Gate is taken over by his nephew, Tsing-ling, who is much less honourable. He adulterates the opium. 'The nephew does things very shabbily… I've found burnt bran in my pipe over and over again. Besides, the room is never cleaned, and all the mats are torn and cut at the edges.'

Misquitta, however, lacks the energy or initiative to go elsewhere. In fact, he would like to die at the Gate, for life is meaningless and he has no ambition. The story ends:

I should like to die—on a clean, cool mat with a pipe of good stuff between my lips. When I feel I'm going, I shall ask Tsing-ling for them, and watch the black and red dragons have their last big fight together; and then …. Well, it doesn't matter. Nothing matters much to me—only I wish Tsing-ling wouldn't put bran into the Black Smoke.

In the story, the original owner of the Gate, Fung-Tching, kept his ornate and splendid coffin, on which 'he had spent a good deal of his savings,' in the den ready for his death. In the Pacific, where I once worked, I knew a Chinese trader who, convinced that he was about to die, spend the last twelve years of his life lying next to his coffin.

Mesmerising evidence

Feeling slightly under the weather recently, I decided to go to bed with a book. I looked on my shelves for a suitable volume and alighted on Harriet Martineau's *Life in the Sick Room*.

My copy once belonged to Henry W Longfellow, the American

poet who in his day was as popular as Tennyson but is now almost unread. Harriet Martineau (1802-76) was also popular in her day as a novelist, pamphleteer, travel writer, and social campaigner but is now even less read than Longfellow.

Always rather sickly and virtually deaf, resorting from an early age to an ear trumpet, Martineau spent the years 1839-44 as an almost bedbound invalid at Tynemouth, in the north of England. Her *Life in the Sick Room* (1844) was the fruit of her experience. It is not certain what was wrong with her: that she had an ovarian cyst is well known, but on the other hand she was restored to good health by a mesmerist, suggesting that in large part her problems were psychological.

During her period of invalidity she became dependent upon opiates. Nothing interested her except the next dose:

I observed, with inexpressible shame, that no details of the perils of empires, or of the starving miseries of thousands of my countrymen, could keep my eye from the watch before me, or detain my attention one second beyond the time when I might have my opiate.

Efforts to give up were unavailing: 'For two years, I wished and intended to dispense with my opiate for once, to try how much there was to bear, and how I should bear it; but I never did… and I have now long given up all thoughts of it.'

Then she tried Mr Spencer Hall, the mesmerist who happened to be visiting Newcastle. With nothing to lose she tried him and tells what happened in her *Letters on Mesmerism* (1845):

Various passes were tried by Mr Hall; the first that appeared effectual, and the most so for some time after, were passes over the head, made from behind,—passes from the forehead to the back of the head, and a little way down the spine. I became sensible of an extraordinary appearance, most unexpected, and wholly unlike anything I had ever conceived of. Something seemed to diffuse itself through the atmosphere,—not like smoke, nor steam, nor haze,—but most like a clear twilight, closing in from the windows and down from the ceiling.

The next day Mr Hall was ill (mesmerist, heal thyself?) and Martineau got her servant to imitate him. 'Within one minute the twilight and phosphoric lights appeared; and in two or three more, a delicious sense of ease spread through me,—a cool comfort, before which all pain and distress gave way, oozing out, as it were, at the soles of my feet. I could no more help exclaiming with pleasure than a person in torture crying out with pain. I became hungry, and ate with relish, for the first time for five years.'

She didn't miss her opiates and soon gave them up altogether.

She described sceptics of mesmerism as having 'minds self-exiled from the region of evidence,' a very good phrase that surely describes us all at times. But what counts as evidence? That, of course, is the difficult question.

Killing Dylan Thomas softly

The idea of the 'poète maudit'—the cursed poet—who drinks, drugs, and misbehaves his way to an early grave is one that is now deeply engraved on our consciousness. Of course, nowadays there are a lot of maudits who are by no means poètes: and where everyone is a bohemian, no one is. But still the image lives on.

Dylan Thomas (1914-53) was a perfect poète maudit. He spent much of his short life in dark bars, inhaling smoke and imbibing beer, often at other people's expense. Until I read David N Thomas's book *Fatal Neglect: Who Killed Dylan Thomas?* I (like most people) had always assumed that he had more or less drunk himself to death. But Mr Thomas's theory is that he died from medical incompetence, and his case is a good one.

Thomas was asthmatic and at post mortem examination was found to have chronic obstructive pulmonary disease also. (Did he have an antritrypsin deficiency? He was well on his way to cirrhosis of the liver as well, with oesophageal varices developing and a somewhat enlarged spleen.)

Thomas was not a well man when, towards the end of October 1953, he went to the United States for another reading tour. He had an exacerbation of bronchitis, his breathing was laboured, and he often felt obliged to take the air outside his room.

At 2 am on 4 November Thomas left his hotel room to seek a drink. He famously boasted on his return an hour and a half later that he had drunk 18 double whiskies, that is to say more than a bottle. But this is unlikely: his tolerance had declined, and he was not drunk. At lunchtime he had two beers.

Later in the day he felt unwell—more unwell than usual—and his American doctor, Milton Feltenstein, visited. In fact he visited him three times in the hotel room on 4 November, each time injecting him with corticotropin and morphine, on the last occasion with 30 mg of morphine. It was after that injection that Thomas sank into the coma from which he never awakened.

Dr Feltenstein appears never to have examined Thomas's chest or to have taken any notice of his cough, breathlessness, and fever but to have assumed that his restlessness was caused by the amount of alcohol he believed, mistakenly, that the poet had drunk and that he was now withdrawing. (Even in 1953 morphine was not the treatment of alcohol withdrawal.)

On Thomas's admission to St Vincent's hospital Dr Feltenstein insisted that his diagnosis was the correct one, though x ray pictures and the autopsy showed pneumonia. Whether Thomas would have survived were it not for Dr Feltenstein's ministrations cannot be known for certain, but surely it is unlikely that his liberality with morphine can have improved the prognosis, to put it mildly.

The author of *Fatal Neglect* alleges a cover-up of Dr Feltenstein by other doctors and by the hospital. I am always somewhat reluctant to accept conspiracy theories, in case I should be seen as a paranoid dupe; besides, we all know that cover-ups (or is it covers-up?) are completely alien to the medical temperament.

Addictive letters

Do men choose philosophies, or philosophies men? A friend of mine, who has thought deeply about the question, thinks it is the latter: by which he means, of course, that it is one's temperament rather than abstract considerations of truth that determines one's world view. A cognate question is whether there is such a thing as the addictive personality, and if so, whether each drug has its corresponding personality. Or is it merely circumstances that addict the addict?

The German writer Hans Fallada (1893–1947, real name Rudolf Ditzen), was a man of multiple addictions, but principally to alcohol and morphine. In his *Short Treatise on the Joys of Morphinism* he describes, in terms similar to those of Thomas De Quincey, the pleasures and pains of opiate addiction.

The short story, written in the first person, describes his search for morphine when he has run out. He tries various doctors, one of whom eventually agrees to give him a dose on condition that he agrees to admit himself into an institution for withdrawal and cure. The doctor locks him in a room after he has given him some morphine and then searches for the keys to his car to take him to the institution. The narrator picks up one of the doctor's books in the room and finds it stamped with his name on the flyleaf; he tears it out for later use as a forged prescription. The doctor puts him into his car but, revived by the morphine, our narrator jumps out and runs away.

Meeting up with a fellow addict who has managed to find a large supply of morphine, the narrator injects himself with some but spills the rest, and has to flee his fellow addict's wrath. He then decides to inject himself with cocaine, under the influence of which he strangles his landlady:

I leap at my landlady and grab her by the throat. I push her blond bulk against the wall, her watery eyes are bulging out stupidly and offensively, her head makes a small, vulgar movement on to her right shoulder and she collapses in a soft pile, her sudden torpor pulling her clear of my hands.

Actually, Fallada did once shoot at his wife, though he missed—unlike William Burroughs, author of *The Naked Lunch*, and another morphine addict. Burroughs shot and killed his wife and then used the family money, which he had hitherto affected to despise, to bribe his way out of prison in Mexico. In fact, Fallada had killed before. In 1911, when he was 17 years old, he had formed a suicide pact with a friend, arranged to appear as a duel. Fallada's friend missed, but Fallada did not: his friend was killed. Fallada then shot himself but did not die. He was subsequently admitted for the first of many times to an asylum.

Clearly, Fallada was not what a normal person might call a normal person. But then he hardly lived through normal times. When he was 16 years old he was severely injured in an accident and started to take painkillers. His brother was killed in the First World War, he lived through the period of hyperinflation in Germany, and the rise and apogee of Nazism. He was courted and imprisoned by Dr Goebbels. He ended his days in the Soviet zone. Not an easy life, then, leaving undecided the question of the addictive personality. Although, personally, I think he had one. His books are marvellous.

Martyrs to an easy life

Considering how trivial are the withdrawal symptoms from opiates (by comparison with those from, say, alcohol), they have given rise to a large literature. Indeed, it may be thought that this literature is itself partly responsible for the suffering caused by withdrawal, because by dramatising that suffering it increases the anticipatory anxiety that is so large a proportion of the pain of opiate withdrawal.

Two French authors of somewhat mixed reputation, Jean Cocteau (1889-1963) and Françoise Sagan (1935-2004), wrote accounts of their withdrawal from opiates undertaken in specialised clinics. By the mere fact of doing so they were investing the process with a significance well above the ordinary. No one, after all, would write a book entitled *My Head Cold: The Story of a Recovery*.

Cocteau published his *Opium: The Diary of a Detoxification* in 1930; in it he claimed, on very dubious grounds, that smoking opium was on a completely different aesthetic and philosophical plane from the vulgar habit of injecting synthetic derivatives of opium. Everyone, I suppose, is inclined to see higher purposes in his or her own vices.

Françoise Sagan published *Toxique*, the diary of her withdrawal from dextromoramide (Palfium), in 1964. I remember the scandal that Sagan caused in our household in the 1950s, when a cousin of mine—a bohemian living in Paris of whom my father did not approve, as she lived among writers and other such riff-raff— introduced Sagan's first novel, *Bonjour Tristesse*, into the house.

Sagan was that perennially disturbing type, the self destructive scion of bourgeois parentage. No illicit substance remained untaken by her; in the course of her lifetime she addicted herself to many such substances. Like most rebels she rebelled in the name of authenticity, that goal that recedes like a mirage in the desert. It does not follow that she was always truthful or endowed with an excess of self knowledge.

Toxique starts with the following statement: 'In the summer of 57, after a car accident, I was for three months the victim of sufficiently severe pains that every day I was given a derivative of morphine called Palfium.'

Considering her history of addicting herself to many other substances in many other circumstances, this does not seem an adequate or even plausible statement of her case.

Oddly enough, these pains did not reappear once the Palfium was withdrawn. She wrote: 'Artificial paradise of no-suffering, I will never know you again. I will never again see [the nurses] Fifi or Felix cleverly decapitate those little ampoules with blue writing, that seem so wise, but which are not.' It is obvious that the suffering of which she speaks here is not physical, caused by injury, but existential.

The use of the passive voice is another giveaway: 'I was sufficiently intoxicated that a stay in a specialised clinic was necessary.' Not: 'I intoxicated myself sufficiently that I decided to stay in a specialised clinic.' Sagan was hooked by Palfium in the same way as a blue marlin was by Ernest Hemingway.

At least she didn't use the trope of chains and slavery that has been current ever since De Quincey and Coleridge. On the other hand, she considered herself some kind of martyr to her own suffering: 'I don't want to be martyrised in this way.'

In what way did her martyrdom manifest itself? According to what she wrote, by her own childish behaviour, caused by withdrawal.

A friendly syringe

Anna Kavan (1901-68) was the great granddaughter of Richard Bright, of Bright's disease (inflammation of the kidneys). She took heroin regularly for more than 30 years, wrote 18 books, and, during the time when she could not make a living by her pen, ran a property development company.

She attributed her prolonged addiction to heroin to her loveless upbringing. In a posthumously published book of stories, *Julia and the Bazooka* (she called her syringe her bazooka), she wrote of herself, in the third person, that 'her personality has been damaged by no love in childhood so that she can't make contact with people or feel at home in the world.'

She also wrote that it was a tennis coach who introduced her to the drug, to improve her serve though it is hard to imagine that a tennis serve would be improved by a shot of heroin.

Whether her childhood was quite as loveless as she later made out is not certain. She grew more bitter about her experiences as she grew older, which is not the same as more accurate. It is true that she was sent away to school early in her childhood and that her father committed suicide by jumping overboard from a ship when she was 14; but her mother was often good to her, and she kept her portrait prominently in her sitting room after her death. She never acknowledged her good fortune in receiving from the age of 18 an allowance equivalent to £40,000 a year.

Kavan (who changed her name by deed poll from Helen Edmonds, née Woods) formed few attachments, her strongest being to one of her doctors, Karl Theodore Bluth. Dr Bluth was a refugee from Nazi Germany who prescribed her heroin until his own death. In *Julia and the Bazooka* we learn that 'Julia likes the doctor as soon as she meets him. He is understanding and kind… He does not want to take her syringe away.' Samuel Taylor Coleridge liked the surgeon James Gillman, with whom he went to live, for more or less the same reason.

What was it that Anna Kavan liked about heroin? It was the blunting of her own awareness. 'She hardly remembers how sad and lonely she used to feel before she had the syringe.'

I have never read a better account of this blunting, deemed desirable by her, than in her short story 'Fog.' Told in the first person, it describes how she drives a car under the influence of heroin: 'I felt calmly contented and peaceful, and there was no need to rush. The feeling was injected, of course… helping me to feel not quite there, as if I was driving the car in my sleep.'

She runs over a young man and kills him. The police stop her and take her to the police station, where a policeman questions her. 'The mask-face across the desk was frowning at me... A mask [that of the young man] had been put out of circulation. So what? A mask wasn't human. It was meaningless, unimportant. The whole thing was unreal.'

But the heroin begins to wear off: 'All I wanted then was for everything to go on as before, so that I could stay deeply asleep, and be no more than a hole in space, not here or anywhere at all, for as long as possible, preferably for ever.'

Of course, oblivion cannot gratify, except in contrast to consciousness.

High anxiety cannabis

English writers came late to cannabis by comparison with the French and Americans. Théophile Gautier published his *Le Club des Hachichins* in 1846 and Fitz Hugh Ludlow *The Hasheesh Eater* in 1857. By contrast the first English book on the subject was *The Confessions of an English Hachich-Eater*, published anonymously in 1884, and now thought to be the work of Sir William Laird Clowes (1856-1905), *Times* correspondent and author of a seven volume history of the British navy.

Sir William writes: 'I dare say that English doctors are for the most part ready to confess that they know very little about this drug.' One of the reasons for this, he says, 'is a difficulty in obtaining potent hachich in England.' But, as he rightly adds, 'that difficulty is not now insuperable.'

Sir William was a great fan of the drug. 'I have found it to be a nepenthes, a sweet bringer of delicious oblivion, and a generous parent of delightful dreams... I hope to enjoy its effects many times again.' And he believed it to be harmless: 'I can conscientiously say that, as far as I know, I am not one whit the worse for my experiences with this delightful drug.'

As the reviewer of the book for the *Edinburgh Courant* put it, 'We would not be surprised if some foolish individuals endeavoured to procure some of the drug, with a view to experiencing the sensations described by the author.'

Sir William has nothing but contempt for the 'Dr Omnibus' who warns him that the drug will weaken his brain.

> *Dr Omnibus, with all my respects, is a fool. It is he who says, 'Don't drink beer—it is adulterated. Don't drink spirits—they destroy the coats of the stomach. Don't drink tea or coffee—it ruins the digestion and deadens the nerves.' In similar strains, he makes onslaughts on tobacco, on corsets, on lobster salads... Do you heed him? Of course not. But we all know that the old gentleman must have something to prattle about.*

Sir William describes cannabis dreams. He had one of them on the way home from visiting a surgeon friend in Hammersmith. He had the sensation of flying through the London streets. One of his fellow pedestrians appeared to him to have, instead of a mere nose, 'a large, red, curiously forked, carrot-like proboscis, which he moved at will, just as the octopus moves its tentacles.' Then

> *... the proboscis was growing at a wonderful rate, shooting out new tentacles with great speed... They were of a bright orange colour, and, in shape, much like attenuated spoons... At last one of the wandering tentacles touched me, and I was tenderly enclosed in a sort of living and pulsating network.*

There is no accounting for taste, of course, but this did not sound to me all that delicious an oblivion or delightful a dream (to quote Sir William). And I could not help thinking of a friend who moved from Hammersmith—and England—when the third person was murdered on the street in which he lived. Could it have been that one or more of the murderers was under the influence of cannabis? My friend did not bother to inquire.

Egyptian smoke

What is it about our daily lives that we should so often wish to escape them, either by travelling, by distracting ourselves furiously in pastimes, or of course by resorting to mind-altering substances?

When I worked on some far-distant Pacific islands, where nature was beneficent and life seemed idyllic, I discovered that youths, if they could, inhaled the fumes of petrol. When I asked them why they did so, they did not say that it was because it made them feel better—on the contrary, it made them feel sick and dizzy. It was because it made them feel different; change, it seems, is desired for its own sake.

In Kate Chopin's short story 'The Egyptian Cigarette,' written in 1897, and first published in *Vogue* some three years later, 'my friend, the Architect' gives the narrator, a woman, some cigarettes that an Egyptian holy man has given him. She retreats to the smoking room of the Architect's house and begins to smoke at exactly five o'clock.

What scenes soon follow! The narrator is crawling across the desert sands, having been abandoned by her Rudolf Valentino-type lover riding away on a camel, because he is tired of her kisses, and wants to go to the city. A vulture soon circles above her, and her mouth and lips are sand-parched. Death is imminent.

Luckily, she finds a river, and there she drinks. There is music in a nearby temple, and fruit, and flowers. Then she wakes from her hallucinatory state, and comes to herself.

The clock strikes a quarter past five when she does. That was quite some cigarette, then! It seems that the increase in the tetrahydrocannibol content of cannabis plants is not quite as recent as we might have supposed, though clearly its action was of shorter duration then than it is nowadays, perhaps because brains were tougher in those days.

When she emerges from her hallucinatory state, the narrator sees that there are five Egyptian cigarettes left still to smoke.

As I looked at the cigarettes in their pale wrappers, I wondered what other visions they might hold for me; what might I not find in their mystic fumes? Perhaps a vision of celestial peace; a dream of hopes fulfilled; a taste of rapture, such as had not entered into my mind to conceive.

Yes, mankind is always dreaming of paradise at threepence a bottle, as De Quincey put it in his *Confessions*: some chemical means by which the sorrows of existence can be put behind it once and for all. But Kate Chopin—or at least her narrator, for it is an elementary mistake to mistake the opinions of a fictional character for those of its author—decides against the experiment and just says no, as every sensible person ought: 'I took the cigarettes and crumpled them between my hands. The light breeze caught up the golden threads and bore them writhing and dancing far out among the maple trees.'

In the end, ordinary, unhallucinated reality is rewarding enough for her. Not so for those who resort to drugs in the hope of making the world and their lives within it seem tolerable, interesting or exciting.

6. Dictators

Doctor Jekyll and Mister Assad

Everyone knows the story of *Dr Jekyll and Mr Hyde*, and understands the moral: that there is, lurking within even the best and most benevolent of us, a ravening beast, an evil monster, that requires very little encouragement to emerge. Whether or not this is literally the case, it is a powerful metaphor for the sudden change in character, usually for the worse, that whole populations, and all the more so, individuals, can undergo.

That is why, perhaps, a book about a doctor, one Dr Bashar Al Assad, written by French journalist Jean-Marie Quéméner, is titled *Doctor Bashar, Mister Assad.* How is it possible, asks the author, that Dr Bashar, 'as charismatic as stale bread,' dreaming of nothing but an ophthalmological career in London, should have become 'today's tyrant, massacring his people, apparently without shame' as Syria's president?

Some of the doctors who pass through London, either in training or to practise there, and who go on to political careers in their homelands, are not necessarily fully persuaded that our style of parliamentary democracy is immediately applicable at home. Even his most fervent admirers, for example, would not have claimed that His Excellency the Life President, Ngwazi ('chief of chiefs') Dr Hastings Kamuzu Banda of Malawi was a fervent democrat.

It was very much to Dr Assad's credit, I think, that he became a member of the finest profession rather than a gilded youth in Syria, as his elder brother did. When he arrived in London to pursue his training and career in ophthalmology, the young Dr Assad behaved with commendable modesty, and was liked by his bosses, his colleagues, and his patients, to whose welfare he was devoted. His only ambition appeared to be ophthalmological; there was nothing in his conduct, timid rather than overbearing, that indicated he was the son of a dictator, much less that he was himself an aspiring dictator (which he wasn't).

His fate was affected, if not sealed exactly, by the death of his elder brother Bassel, hitherto the heir-apparent to the dictatorship, in a car crash. Bashar became the heir, and returned to Damascus. His father died in 2000. Dr Assad was thrust into a role that he had not at first sought to play.

From then on, however, by the logic of the situation, he was transformed, from nice Dr Jekyll into nasty Mr Hyde; and what changed him was not Jekyll's potion, 'of reddish hue,' but power.

Hyde displays 'a sort of murderous mixture of timidity and boldness'; precisely how Assad is described after his ascent. Assad also resembled Dr Jekyll, for he was: 'inclined by nature to industry, fond of the respect of the wise and good among [his] fellow-men, and thus, as might have been supposed, with every guarantee of an honourable and distinguished future.'

But a change came over Jekyll thanks to the potion: [He] had been safe of all men's respect, wealthy, beloved... and now [he] was the common quarry of mankind, hunted, houseless, a known murderer, thrall to the gallows.' More and more, Hyde took over from Jekyll: 'The powers of Hyde seemed to have grown with the sickliness of Jekyll.'

Truly, life imitates art.

The Arab spring

There is something fascinating about the memoirs of the servants or confidants of great dictators. They allow us to see raw power close up, and to thrill to its horror. Personally, I can never resist a book with the title *I Was X's Y*, where X was a dictator and Y was his maid, secretary, or chauffeur.

Doctors have written memoirs of dictators. Among the most famous, or infamous, are those of Dr Li Zhisui, *The Private Life of*

Chairman Mao. When they were published there was a controversy as to how genuine they were, with both translator and publisher accused of spicing them up to attract sales. The author himself was accused of claiming a closer relationship than he really had with the Great Helmsman, whose insatiable sexual appetite and deficient personal hygiene, an unfortunate combination, he describes in horrifying detail.

Hitler's doctor, Theodor Morell, kept a secret diary in which he recorded his master's manifold symptoms and his unconventional treatment of them (he was known sarcastically as the chief Reich injection officer)—treatment which is thought by many to have hastened Hitler's physical deterioration. Once in US captivity, Morell himself claimed to have applied such treatment precisely for that end; but then he would, wouldn't he?

Franco's dentist, Julio Gonzalez Iglesias, wrote a memoir called *Los Dientes de Franco (Franco's Teeth)*, a dental biography of the Caudillo, in which we learn the effect Franco's continual dental problems—he suffered greatly from toothache—had upon his temper and hence upon his decisions.

It is not surprising that even those memoirs of dictators not written by doctors should contain medical details of some importance. For example, I read *In the Shadow of the Queen*, the memoirs of Lotfi Ben Chrouda, butler to Zine El Abidine Ben Ali, the deposed Tunisian dictator. The author served the president and attended to the vulgar pharaonic whims of Leila Trabelsi, Ben Ali's second wife, for more than 20 years. According to his coauthor, the Tunisian journalist, Isabelle Soares Boumalala, 'the past still weighs on Ben Chrouda, but he began to free himself from Leila from the first day of the revelations he made for this book, which was a kind of release for him.'

According to the butler, the balance of power between husband and wife changed in her favour as he became ill, and it was Leila Trabelsi's unbounded kleptocratic ambition that caused the downfall of the regime and the hatred of the population. Ben Ali had cancer of the prostate and was treated with chemotherapy, administered by German doctors, which made him look so weak and ill that he had to be heavily made up every time he appeared in public; he began to dement at more or less the same time. When he fled Tunisia, he could hardly grasp any more where he was or what was happening around him.

As with all palace memoirs, no one knows how much of this is true. Some say that the book is a long exercise in self justification, that the author benefited from the regime, and now that it has fallen ignominiously wants to present himself as a prisoner or victim of it rather than a collaborator. But if his story is true, then Ben Ali's illness had a profound effect on world history. For no prostate cancer and dementia, no ascendancy of Leila Trabelsi; no ascendancy of Leila Trabelsi, no Tunisian revolution; and no Tunisian revolution, no Arab spring.

Doctors and the dictator

In his review of Rengger and Longchamp's *Historical Essay on the Paraguayan Revolution and the Dictatorship of Doctor Francia*, Thomas Carlyle, who from the safety of Cheyne Row, Chelsea, was much in favour of the said dictator, whom he greatly admired, wrote: 'The Messrs Rengger and Longchamp were, and we hope still are, two Swiss surgeons; who in the year 1819 resolved on carrying their talents into South America, into Paraguay, with views towards 'natural history,' among other things.'

The heavy sarcasm disguises an inaccuracy. The Swiss surgeons said in their book (actually written by Rengger alone) that they were primarily interested in natural history and hoped to keep themselves by practising medicine. They were not interested in other things; Carlyle's insinuation that they were was nothing but a smear and a sneer.

Having entered Paraguay, Rengger and Longchamp found that they could not leave it. Doctor Francia, closed the borders; no one was allowed to enter or to leave the country. Rengger and Longchamp became physicians to the dictator (whose doctorate was in theology) and his troops.

Spies were everywhere; Francia had the trees of Asunción cut down in case they should conceal assassins and unrolled the cigars his sister made for him in case she had inserted something dangerous (other than tobacco, of course). Passers-by could be shot for looking too long in the direction of the dictator's residence, for he had given instructions that his guards should shoot on sight. If they missed, they were to shoot again. If they missed a second time, they were in turn to be shot.

Once, Francia asked Rengger to perform a postmortem examination to see whether Paraguayans had an anatomical peculiarity in their necks that prevented them from looking him in the eye.

Having detained them for six years, Francia finally let the two doctors leave Paraguay. He was not pleased when they published their book relating his atrocities. With all the fury of a dictator calumniated, he published a refutation in a newspaper in Buenos Aires: 'Rengger occupied himself in the poisoning of such American patients as he could lay hold of… During the two months in which Rengger attended the barracks of the regiment of men of colour, he despatched more than 20 of them, and was on this account sent about his business; when at once the mortality ceased. Adieu, pill-doctor!—Adieu, purger! —Adieu, poisoner!'

Rengger and Longchamp's book was the only one about Francia until, 12 years later, the Robertson brothers published *Francia's Reign of Terror*. They were held captive in Paraguay for four years; in their book they mention an English doctor, Dr Parlett: 'Very clever in his profession, but unfortunately of very dissipated habits.' He quickly distinguished himself after his arrival in the country from the Spanish doctors, who were known as 'matasanos' (killers of the healthy), and produced many marvellous cures, including the extraction from a young girl's eye of a jigger that was blinding her.

Francia's refusal to let Dr Parlett leave the country drove him to drink even more than he would have in any case. He died in Paraguay,

> *… one of many men of abilities whom I have known in South America who, released from the moral restraint to which they have been accustomed at home, and without sufficient energy of character to resist temptation, have sunk to their graves unheeded and unlamented, instead of being followed to them by good men sorrowing over departed worth and talent.*

No remedies left

The worst dictatorships try to destroy not only people but memory itself; and among the worst dictatorships in a century full of dictatorships was that of Ahmed Sékou Touré, president of the West African state of Guinea for more than a quarter of the 20th century. A third of a population fled his rule, and many thousands were tortured and killed, victims of the dictator's paranoia.

A Guinean doctor, Mandiouf Mauro Sidibe, has recently published a book, *La fin de Sékou Touré (The End of Sékou Touré)*, which tries to preserve an aspect of that dark period of his country's history. He has kept and transcribed the radio commentary that accompanied the dictator's state funeral, which was attended by many heads of state and government. At this time sycophancy was still the safest policy for Guineans, a sycophancy so extravagant that it was possible only in conditions of extreme terror.

The funeral oration in the stadium given by his successor would have been comic if it were not for the fact that scarcely a family in the country had not lost someone to the insatiable lust for power of the Great Departed, as he was known for a time.

'Eternal glory to President Ahmed Sékou Touré! [the funeral oration began] Eternal glory to President Ahmed Sékou Touré! Eternal glory to President Ahmed Sékou Touré!' It continued:

Heroic people of Guinea, Ahmed Sékou Touré, to whom today you render your last homage in serenity, order, discipline, and cleanliness of body, heart, and mind, is going to do what he will never do again, take the tour of honour round the stadium, in the atmosphere of the great popular demonstrations which he galvanised as soon as he entered the crowd, amidst the prolonged ovations of his militants, all enthusiasts, giving rise or responding to the very communicative smile of the Supreme Director of the Revolution and the movement, so familiar to the people of Guinea, or to the white handkerchief from which the image of President Ahmed Sékou Touré is inseparable... Where, then, Comrade President, are your smile, your optimism that every one of us loved, that remedy for so many ills? Where, then, is your white handkerchief, Comrade President? Wave it to give us back hope.

A week after the death of the 'universal genius and giant of history mourned by the people of the whole world' there was a coup d'état. The radio broadcasts then spoke of his ruthless and bloody dictatorship, vowed to rid the country of feudalism, corruption, and the abuse of power, and promised to release all political prisoners from their camps.

Sékou Touré had left the country in such a state that he himself was a victim of it, Dr Sidibe tells us. During his final illness there was no equipment or drugs in the country with which to treat him. He was flown to the Cleveland Clinic, but he died soon after arrival. Dr Sidibe quotes an African proverb: 'When you dig your enemy's grave, do not dig it too deep, or you risk falling into it yourself.'

Dr Sidibe finishes his book by recounting the last illnesses that he witnessed of two people 10 years later, one who was tortured and one who was a torturer during the dictatorship. The first died in peace and tranquillity; the other was torn between fear and aggression and actually bit one of the nurses looking after him. Fearing that the staff of the hospital would take revenge on him, he left for a foreign country where no one knew him. There he died.

This little book of Dr Sidibe's is one of quiet heroism.

Selections

It is an old adage that we should count our blessings, and it is an equally ancient failing of human beings that they should fail to do so. For we are as much problem seeking as problem solving creatures, and we soon feel wretched if we have nothing to complain about.

My wife and I once visited a missionary doctor in Haiti called Dr Hodges. I had met him there 10 years earlier, when he told me that he wished to retire soon in Haiti and concentrate on archaeology. (He had discovered the place where Christopher Columbus had first landed and founded a small museum.) But when we met him again the medical needs of the population had grown so much that, though well into his 70s, he had not been able to retire. We found him, exhausted, in the middle of triage, surrounded by hundreds of patients. We resolved thereafter, whenever either of us complained of some trivial frustration in the NHS, to say to the other, 'Remember Dr Hodges.'

Our resolution lasted about two weeks, but I experienced the same sense of shame about my own thinness of skin recently when reading Primo Levi's first published work 'Auschwitz Report', an article he wrote in partnership with a fellow inmate of Auschwitz, Leonardo de Benedetti. Dr de Benedetti was a general practitioner from Turin who, with his wife, was turned back at the border when they tried to reach Switzerland and were later deported to Auschwitz, his wife being killed immediately. Levi and de Benedetti were among the thousand inmates remaining in the camp when the Russians arrived.

'Auschwitz Report' was written at the request of the Russians and published in 1946 in the Turin medical journal *Minerva Medica*. It concerns the medical conditions and 'services' in that part of Auschwitz where inmates were kept who were still capable of working for the artificial rubber plant established there. De Benedetti, who was 21 years older than Levi—that is to say 45 when he was sent to the camp—survived four 'selections,' the process by which those who were deemed too ill to work were sent off for extermination.

De Benedetti returned with Levi to Italy, where he worked as a doctor until he was 80 years old. When he died five years later, Levi wrote two brief and moving encomiums to him. De Benedetti had looked after Levi when he had pneumonia, Levi wrote, and

> ... *his kindly and indomitable character, his infectious capacity for hope, and his zeal as a medical practitioner with no medicines were invaluable not only to us, the very few survivors of Auschwitz, but to thousands of other Italian men and women on the uncertain journey back from exile.*

De Benedetti, who never remarried,

> ... *did not enjoy solitude, and at first he lived with relatives and then with a family of friends: Dr Arrigo Vita and his two sisters. They passed away one after another, and Dr de Benedetti was left on his own. Until he was 80, he had been the hard-working and highly esteemed doctor of the rest home, where*

he decided to take up residence in the serene sadness of one who knows he has not lived in vain.

How many of us will be able on our death beds to say the same?

Hiding and hauntings

Spy stories, with few exceptions, fail to excite me; I prefer a good murder any day. But one of the most gripping books I have ever read was by Joseph Kessel, *Les Mains du miracle*, translated into English as *The Magic Touch* or, in the United States, as *The Miraculous Hands*. It is about Heinrich Himmler's personal doctor, Felix Kersten.

Kessel (1898–1979), like so many writers the son of a doctor, was born in Argentina and brought up for a few years in Russia before his family moved to France. He was an adventurer on a grand scale and wrote scores of books. Decorated in the First World War, he joined the French resistance in the second. After the war, he heard about Dr Kersten, then living in Sweden. He interviewed him for many days, and wrote a documentary fiction about him, which was published with a preface by Hugh Trevor-Roper in 1961, shortly after Kersten's death.

Kersten was Finnish, though born in Estonia when it was still part of the Russian Empire; he fought against the Soviets in 1919 and afterwards became a masseur in the Finnish army. He studied medicine in Germany but became a disciple of Dr Ko, a Chinese masseur (who also qualified in Western medicine in London) who used ancient Tibetan techniques of massage.

Dr Kersten soon built up a large clientele in Germany—for example, healing a famous industrialist who was so grateful that he gave him a fee big enough to buy a large estate.

Himmler, who had intermittent but excruciating abdominal cramps that no doctor could relieve, heard about Dr Kersten and consulted him. Kersten's magic touch relieved Himmler's suffering as nothing else could, and Kersten became Himmler's trusted confidant. Kersten used his position to intervene with Himmler to save hundreds and ultimately thousands of lives.

According to Kessel's book, Kersten used his power over

Himmler's abdominal cramps to act as a spy for the Swedish, Finnish, and Dutch governments in exile and to get him to abandon his plan to deport the whole population of the Netherlands to Poland. He told Himmler that his cramps would not yield even to his treatment while he, Himmler, was trying both to increase the size of the SS to more than one million members and work on the planned deportation; it was too much for his nervous system. Kersten told Himmler that he had to abandon one or the other if the massage to relieve his symptoms was to work; and he knew that increasing the size of the SS was more important. Himmler did abandon the plan to deport all the Dutch. However, no proof that such a plan existed has ever been found.

Certainly part of the Kessel-Kersten story is true; there is documentary evidence that Dr Kersten intervened to save many lives. However, some doubts creep in. Dr Kersten is portrayed in the book as playing on Himmler's weakness for charcuterie; but Himmler was a strict vegetarian.

What was Himmler's chronic condition, whose recurring acute exacerbations could be completely relieved time after time by Dr Kersten's 'miraculous hands,' and by nothing else? Even opiates had failed to relieve Himmler's pain. Kessel expresses no interest in the question; he accepts Kersten's story at face value and expresses no scepticism towards it. But the book is so well written that it carries you along with it. I challenge you to put it down once taken up.

Let's look at rationality

Theodor Gomperz (1832-1912) was a great Austrian classicist who impressed and was impressed by Freud: indeed it was he who commissioned Freud to translate a volume of John Stuart Mill's work into German. Gomperz's son, a philosopher, was a patient of Freud's for a time.

Gomperz devoted a chapter in his great four volume history of classical philosophy to the Greek doctors, especially to Hippocrates and the school of Cos. He was extremely complimentary about them, seeing them as forerunners not only of rational medicine but of a properly empirical and scientific approach to the phenomena of nature as a whole.

To Gomperz primitive medicine was merely absurd: 'As well as magic spells, amulets, and various ceremonies, medicinal plants and ointments were used, and it was not rare that a single, unique remedy was used against the most diverse diseases.' There was certainly nothing rational about it:

The fantastic element was so great that the choice of medicines was determined as much by an association of ideas as by actual experience. The red colour of haematite seemed to have destined it for haemostasis. In Egypt, it was believed that the blood of black animals would prevent hair from turning white; while today in Styria, as once in India, Greece and Italy, the bodies of yellow birds were thought to expel jaundice.

Gomperz compares this farrago of nonsense with the rationality of the Hippocratic corpus. Praising the author of *Airs, Waters, Places,* he says:

The author is a man whose foot had trodden the soil of southern Russia as well as that of the Nile Valley, whose scrutinising eye had surveyed an infinite and inexhaustible variety of scenes and whose powerful mind tried to combine this immense mass of detail into a single pattern. But his precious observations, and his numerous but premature conjectures on the relation between climate and health, between the succession of seasons and the course of illnesses, were as nothing compared with the immortal honour of having been the first to try to establish a causative relation between the character of peoples and the physical conditions in which they live.

He likewise praises the author of *On the Sacred Malady* (epilepsy), who denied the divine nature of the falling sickness and who wrote: 'The nature and cause of this illness derives from precisely the same divine principle that gives rise to all the rest. None is more divine, none is more human, than any other.'

For Gomperz this was a great advance in rationality, because if everything was equally divine it followed that everything could be investigated with equal empirical rigour.

Not having lived to see the First World War, Gomperz believed that empirical knowledge inevitably led to 'a fully rational life,' a better existence, which perhaps explains why the question of whether the Greeks actually benefited from Hippocratic rationality at the time of Hippocrates never so much as crossed his mind. It seemed sufficient to him that Hippocrates was an intellectual forerunner, albeit a distant one, of the current state of enlightenment: but when we read the medical texts of Gomperz's day, with their floating kidneys leading to nephroplexy, and their autointoxications leading to hemicolectomies (partial colon removal), we realise how far rationality had to go before it reached its apogee—in us, of course.

7. Ideas

The life of crowds

The behaviour of people in crowds is rather different from that of the same people in the privacy of their own homes; so much is obvious. But it was the French doctor, writer, and all round intellectual Gustave Le Bon (1841-1931) who was the first to consider the difference at book length. His *Psychology of Crowds*, published in 1895, was a founding text of social psychology.

Le Bon is usually said to have qualified as a doctor in Paris in 1866, though some have disputed whether he ever passed his baccalaureat, let alone his doctorate. Be that as it may, he practised for a time and published widely on such medical matters as premature burial, venereal disease, and the composition of tobacco smoke. He also published *Anatomical and Mathematical Researches on Variations in the Volume of the Brain and their Relation to Intelligence.*

He gave up the practice of medicine to write travel books and histories of several ancient civilisations. He was also an amateur physicist, claiming to have discovered the theory of relativity before Einstein. There are few doubts about the range of his interests; he was known and respected by all the leading French intellectuals of his day.

But it is on his study of crowd psychology that his fame now rests. Freud read it; Le Bon popularised the concept of the unconscious before Freud did. Both Lenin and Hitler read the book closely, and it is strange indeed that Hitler did not recognise himself in the less than admiring portrait of the leader of crowds that Le Bon paints:

Leaders are generally not men of thought but of action. They are not lucid, and cannot be, for lucidity leads to doubt. They are recruited among the neurotics, the hotheads, the semi-psychotics who are on the fringes of madness. All reasoning is blunted by their conviction, however absurd the ideas that they promote or the ends that they pursue. Contempt and persecution only strengthen their determination. Personal and family interests, all are sacrificed. The survival instinct itself is absent in them, to the point at which the only reward that they seek is martyrdom. The sheer strength of their conviction lends a suggestive power to their words.

Le Bon's populariser in Britain was also a medical man, Wilfred Trotter, professor of surgery at University College Hospital, whose *Instincts of the Herd in Peace and War* was inspired by the *Psychology of Crowds*.

According to Le Bon, prejudice and gusts of emotion have a greater influence on crowds (in which he includes juries and electorates) than evidence, reason, and logic, which are weak weapons indeed.

A pall of unrespectability has always hovered over Le Bon, not only because he spread himself intellectually thin over a wide range but because—undoubted racist as he was—he is suspected of being a forerunner of fascism. This is not quite fair, however; he was describing reality as he saw it, not approving or extolling it. Indeed, he lamented it. But could anyone who has listened to successful modern politicians deny that they use unsupported assertion and repetition more than reason and evidence, just as Le Bon says? And who could gainsay his advice to all public speakers: that the most, the only, effective defence against calumny is to calumniate the calumniator?

The wages of conformity

Great works of literature have meanings beyond the most obvious, and judged by this standard Max Frisch's play *The Fire Raisers* is a great work. Frisch was a Swiss who worked for a number of years as an architect before turning full time to writing. No doubt unfairly, we do not normally associate the Swiss with literature: who ever uses the phrase 'Swiss literature,' for example? Nor do we expect the best societies always to produce the best literature; for what is good for people is not necessarily good for writing.

In *The Fire Raisers*, an entire town is subject to a rash of arson attacks, so that everyone is terrified by the prospect of further attacks. The action of the play takes place in the home of Herr Biedermann, a rich bourgeois who makes his money from the manufacture and sale of fake hair restorative. Two dubious characters, Schmitz and Eisenring, take up residence in Herr Biedermann's attic. He does not want them there, but is too cowardly and pusillanimous to evict them.

Gradually, they make it clear to Herr Biedermann that they are the arsonists of whom the town is afraid. They move drums of petrol into the attic; they ask Herr Biedermann for help with the fuse with which they are going to light the fire; they even ask him, successfully, for the matches with which to start it.

Throughout the preparation of the fire, Herr Biedermann— though he hates, fears and despises Schmitz and Eisenring, and again through cowardice and pusillanimity—refuses to accept the evidence before his eyes.

Eisenring explains Schmitz's uncouth behaviour by his unhappy childhood, and Herr Biedermann, through sentimentality rather than from real sympathy, feels unable to answer. He invites the two interlopers to a dinner of goose stuffed with chestnuts (before accepting the invitation, Eisenring makes sure there is to be red cabbage also), and though the two are complete ruffians, they insist that the best silver, including finger bowls, be laid on a damask tablecloth. After dinner, they burn the house down, and the final scene takes place in Hell, where Herr Biedermann and his wife protest their innocence.

Frisch, of course, lived through the Nazi takeover of Germany, but saw it from the German-speaking fringe. It doesn't take much historical knowledge to understand that he is writing about the Nazi era, but not just about the Nazi era: his play is about the perpetual human temptation not to see, and then to compromise with evil.

Eisenring tells Herr Biedermann the secret of his success (but still Herr Biedermann disguises the truth from himself):

Joking is the third best method of hoodwinking people. The second best is sentimentality. The kind of stuff [Schmitz] goes in for—an orphanage, and so on. But the best and safest method—in my opinion—is to tell the plain unvarnished truth. Oddly enough. No one believes it.

And Hitler, as we know, did not do anything that he did not say he was going to do in *Mein Kampf*.

What has all this to do with us, you ask. Well, a friend of mine was recently told by a manager of no clinical experience whatever that, by such and such a date, such and such a number of patients should have been on such and such a drug for such and such a period of time. If not, funding would decline.

Sometimes I wonder whether we in the medical profession have been, in our own small way, a pack of Herr Biedermanns.

One's own health

The unexamined life, or so we are told on the reliable evidence of Socrates, is not worth living. The question then becomes whether the examined life is worth living either.

Hypochondriasis is one way of leading the examined life. It is often claimed that many medical students, on first opening clinical textbooks, fall prey in their imaginations to the maladies that they read about, though I must admit that I have not noticed any excessive nervousness about health among such students.

Jerome K Jerome famously describes the effect of reading textbooks of diseases on the minds of the susceptible in the opening of *Three Men in a Boat*:

I remember going to the British Museum one day to read up the treatment for some slight ailment of which I had a touch—hay fever, I fancy it was. I got down the book, and read all I came to read; and then, in an unthinking moment, I idly turned the leaves, and began to indolently study diseases, generally. I forget which was the first distemper I plunged into—some fearful, devastating scourge, I know—and, before I had glanced half down the list of 'premonitory symptoms,' it was borne in upon me that I had fairly got it.

I sat for awhile, frozen with horror; and then, in the listlessness of despair, I again turned over the pages. I came to typhoid fever—read the symptoms— discovered that I had typhoid fever, must have had it for months without knowing it—wondered what else I had got; turned up St Vitus's Dance— found, as I expected, that I had that too—began to get interested in my case, and determined to sift it to the bottom, and so started alphabetically—read up ague, and learnt that I was sickening for it, and that the acute stage would commence in about another fortnight. Bright's disease, I was relieved to find, I had only in a modified form, and, so far as that was concerned, I might live for years. Cholera I had, with severe complications; and diphtheria I seemed to have been born with.

Addison, in *The Spectator*, described precisely the same process nearly 200 years before, in 1711. He received a letter from a man who described himself as 'one of that sickly tribe who are commonly known by the name of valetudinarians.' His correspondent continued: 'I first contracted this ill habit of body, or rather of mind, by the study of physic. I no sooner began to pursue books of this nature, but I found my pulse was irregular; and scarce ever read the account of any disease that I did not fancy myself afflicted with.'

A friend of mine has long contended that we need freedom from opinion at least as much as we need freedom of opinion, and perhaps the same might be said of freedom of and from information. Those of my readers who have experienced patients arriving with reams of paper downloaded from the internet will doubtless know what I mean.

I do not know the answer to hypochondriasis, but Addison quotes Martial's description of perfect happiness: the state of neither fearing nor wishing for death. And I remember with admiration a friend—a very distinguished man who, it was said, undeservedly missed a Nobel Prize—who in his 80s told me that, of all subjects, he found that of his own health the least interesting.

Stuffings

In Jerome K Jerome's *Three Men in a Boat*, the author (and narrator) had seemed to have practically every symptom of every disease (except housemaid's knee).

He explained his plight to his friend and doctor, who examined him and handed him a prescription that the author duly took to the chemist's. The chemist looked at it and said that he could not fill it. The reason was in the nature of the prescription:

1 lb beefsteak, with
1 pt bitter beer every 6 hours
1 ten-mile walk every morning
1 bed at 11 sharp every night

This came with an added injunction: 'And don't stuff up your head with things you don't understand.'

I doubt that we would dare say such a thing to anyone, even a friend, nowadays, let alone commit it to writing as documentary evidence of our attitude.

Medical students early in their clinical studies, it is said, suffer from what might be called the Jerome K Jerome syndrome: on reading of diseases, they imagine they have one or other of them. I never suffered from this but rather the opposite, a strong notion that illness was what happened to other people. So much did I have this notion that when as a young doctor I experienced a strange sensation I had difficulty in putting a name to it, though in fact it was breathlessness. Soon the unmistakable symptoms of pneumonia made themselves evident: not only was my lung attacked but also my sense of invulnerability. It has been attacked several times since.

Jerome K Jerome was what might be called a sucker for patent medicines too. He had only to see the list of symptoms supposedly caused by disorders of the liver and cured by liver pills to realise that he had been suffering from liver all his life. For example, 'a general disinclination to work of any kind,' a cardinal symptom, had been with him since an early age. 'As a boy, the disease hardly left me for a day. They did not know, then, that it was my liver. Medical science was in a far less advanced state than now, and they used to put it down to laziness.'

He didn't get liver pills but a cuff round the ear. It produced a symptomatic improvement for a time, but the disease always returned.

Jerome K Jerome once inadvertently assisted me in uncovering a KGB spy. A naturalised Russian friend of mine who, having attended the Foreign Languages Institute in Moscow, speaks the most perfect English, once referred in a conversation to Jerome Jerome.

'Aha!' I said. 'Now I know that you are a KGB agent, which I had always suspected. No native Briton would call him Jerome Jerome. By missing out his initial'—which, incidentally, stands for Klapka, the Hungarian general who was staying in the house in Walsall where the author was born—'you have revealed yourself as a plant.'

I think Jerome K Jerome would have liked that.

Our acquaintance with death

What fails to happen is sometimes as important as what does happen. This is most famously (and felicitously) expressed in Dr Conan Doyle's story *Silver Blaze*:

> *'Is there anything to which you would like to draw my attention?'*
> *'To the curious incident of the dog in the night-time.'*
> *'The dog did nothing in the night-time.'*
> *'That was the curious incident,' remarked Sherlock Holmes.*

Likewise, as every married couple knows, what is unsaid is often as important as what is said. And what historians omit from, or do not emphasise in, their accounts of the past tells us much about the mentality of their own times.

In the philosopher David Hume's *The History of England from the Invasion of Julius Caesar to the Revolution of 1688*, we are told that in the year 1349, in the middle of the Hundred Years' War, Edward III instituted the Order of the Garter with considerable fanfare. But, Hume continues:

> *... a sudden damp was thrown over the festivity... by a destructive pestilence which invaded the kingdom, as well as the rest of Europe, and is computed*

to have swept away nearly a third of the inhabitants in every country which it attacked. It was probably more fatal in great cities than in the country; and above fifty thousand souls are said to have perished in London alone... So great a calamity, more than the pacific dispositions of the princes, served to maintain and prolong the peace between France and England.

And that, in effect, is the only thing Hume has to say on the subject of an epidemic that caused the death of a third of the population.

This is not a view of history that would find much favour today. We live in an age of obsession with health, when the deaths of a few people are sufficient to spark a panic worldwide. How could Hume have passed over the Black Death with such apparent unconcern and equanimity?

One possible explanation is that he was callous and indifferent to the fate of the great mass of mankind. I do not think this is very likely, however, for few people who knew him had anything bad to say of Hume. In his letter to William Strachan about their mutual friend, Adam Smith says: 'Upon the whole, I have always considered him [Hume]... as approaching as nearly the idea of a perfectly wise and virtuous man, as perhaps the nature of human frailty will admit.'

Since both Hume and Smith wrote feelingly of the benefits of human sympathy, and made it indeed the basis of their moral philosophy, it is unlikely that Hume was merely hard hearted when he wrote so little of the Black Death.

I remember reading a book a long time ago about the London of Hume's day by Dorothy M George. A single statistic so startled me that I have never forgotten it: that a half of all children in the London of that time died before the age of 5. If it had not been for the constant influx of people from outside the city, the population of London would have fallen rather than risen.

In these circumstances, everyone in Hume's day must have had a close personal acquaintance with death, and therefore the events of 1349 must have seemed correspondingly less terrible than to us, who have so much difficulty in grasping the fact of our own mortality.

The art of special pleading

Whenever I feel sorry for myself, which is not infrequently, I try to think of those less fortunate than I am—who, after all, are the great mass of the world's population. This technique, I am ashamed to say, seldom works; I still feel just as sorry for myself as before.

Nevertheless, I should recommend everyone inclined to the vice of self pity, especially doctors, to read John Vaizey's *Scenes from Institutional Life*, a brief memoir of the author's two years during the war spent in hospital being treated for osteomyelitis (infection) of the spine. Vaizey (1929-84) triumphed over the most terrible suffering to become an eminent university professor of economics and member of the House of Lords.

He was 14 when he felt acute pain in his spine and fell very ill. He was taken to a hospital that he does not name, where for a long time he was expected to die, and would gladly have done so. Indeed, he was put in a side ward where he might die out of sight of the other patients. The hospital ward was terrible:

An old Greek gentleman would come down the ward to speak to me. He told me that my screams [of pain] had terrorized them all. Then he died. Another old gentleman fought to get out of bed every night. They boarded him in. One night he threw himself out and when they picked him up he was dead. One night the man opposite me, who was not allowed to drink because he had a perforated duodenal ulcer, drank his mouthwash and died with a gurgle, after a bout of prolonged screaming.

Vaizey's deep wounds after several operations were unpacked and packed without pain relief; he developed foot drop; he had painful enemas (in public) every other day. The continual pus from his wounds and sores smelt foul. In the circumstances:

I used to look forward to air-raids. Then the beds would be pulled into the middle of the wards and the windows would be opened to allow the blast to pass through the ward. The curtains would blow back and the flashes of the guns and the movements of the searchlights would become clear. The fear and terror outside matched that inside my mind, my own chaos responded to the other chaos.

The special requests of the patients were often met with the argument, 'If I do it for you I have to do it for all'—this, of course, being impossible.

There was a fantastic levelling-down quality about the spirit of the hospital which made an individuality difficult to assert. It was, of course, an argument from stupidity; if the need were reasonable it should have been satisfied for all, and if it were not suitable for all then it was extremely likely they wouldn't want it.

Alas, Vaizey's entirely understandable revulsion against the way in which he was treated in hospital drove him to an absurd utopianism, according to which we had no need of institutions. He was like a man who goes to a library and, finding it does not have the book he wants, concludes that libraries are not needed. To say that 'institutions give inadequate people what they want—power' is at best a very partial truth (surely everyone will recognise that it is sometimes true, perhaps increasingly so).

Suffering, then, can overcome reason many years after it occurred, even in the most intelligent.

Memento mori

Like many a famous author, Walter Scott (1771-1832) had a doctor in the family: his maternal grandfather, John Rutherford, who studied in Leiden, was awarded his degree at Rheims, became professor of physic at Edinburgh, was the first man in Britain to teach medicine to students at the bedside, and delivered his lectures in Latin, in which language he was said to be more fluent than in his native tongue.

John Gibson Lockhart's *Life of Sir Walter Scott* is often said to be the second greatest literary biography in English, (long) after Boswell, of course. At the beginning of the work is a short memoir of his early life by Scott himself, which is of considerable medical interest.

It was written before the passage of the Anatomy Act, when the only source of bodies for dissection was the hangman's noose or those feloniously resurrected from recent interment. Sir Walter tells us that if his life were of use in moral instruction he 'would as readily consent to [a minute narrative of] it as I would bequeath my body to dissection, if the operation should tend to point out the nature and the means of curing any peculiar malady.' Considering how unpopular and feared human dissection was at the time, this was a very enlightened attitude.

Scott was one of 12 children, only five of whom survived infancy. One of his surviving brothers joined the East India Company 'and died a victim of the climate,' that is to say from a disease such as malaria. His sister Anne was accident prone, and when she was aged 6 her cap caught fire and burnt her severely. Scott wrote that this made her delicate all her life, 'the slightest cold occasioning swellings in her face,' and she died aged only 29. Another brother died on his return from the West Indies.

Then Sir Walter describes what happened to him when he was 18 months old: 'One night, I shewed great reluctance to be caught and put to bed; and after being chased about the room, was apprehended and consigned to my dormitory with some difficulty. It was the last time I was to shew such personal agility. In the morning, I was discovered to be afflicted with the fever which often accompanies the cutting of large teeth. It held me three days. On the fourth, they discovered that I had lost the power of my right leg.'

This relatively mild case of polio was perhaps of some use to the development of Scott's literary career, for, being unable to compete at school in games, he compensated in the search for popularity by developing a skill in telling stories.

Many remedies were tried on him. His grandfather, the professor of medicine, proving powerless, a folk remedy was resorted to: wrapping him up in the warm skin of a recently slaughtered sheep. This did not work either, nor did a prolonged stay in Bath.

Polio was not the only near escape that Scott had as a child. His nurse 'contracted a sort of hatred at poor me,' and she confessed that one day she 'carried me up to the [hills] under a strong temptation of the Devil, to cut my throat with her scissors, and bury me in the moss.' Scott adds with admirable restraint: 'She was dismissed, of course, and I have heard became afterwards a lunatic.'

Echo chambers

Henry James once remarked that an excessive interest in the works of Edgar Allan Poe was the sign of a primitive sensibility: such as Baudelaire's, I suppose. I cannot but agree with James on this point, and I might add that Poe's prose style seems to me dense without depth and earnest without seriousness.

One of Poe's preoccupations was shared by many people of his time, namely premature burial. Throughout the 19th century, and even into the beginning of the 20th century, books appeared about the danger of precocious interment, with advice as to how to avoid it. There was even a Society for the Prevention of Burial Before Death, which published many books and pamphlets; it made much of the fact that death was a difficult diagnosis, the subject of controversy among doctors. (*Romeo and Juliet* would not have been a tragedy without a mistaken diagnosis of death.)

Indeed, the precautions against burial alive taken by Poe's narrator in the story 'The Premature Burial' are precisely those recommended in *Premature Burial and How It May Be Prevented*, second edition 1905, by William Tebb and Edward Perry Vellum MD. Tebb was not a doctor, but he was interested in such good causes as the abolition of slavery and the avoidance of premature burial, to which cause he gave the last years of his life. He was also the originator and propagator of the idea that leprosy was caused by smallpox vaccination, and wrote a lengthy treatise on this subject. Dr Vellum had been medical inspector of the US Army and became interested in the subject of premature burial after he nearly drowned, was given up for dead, and woke up just before his own interment. Tebb's book is full of lurid stories that make the flesh creep:

In a small town in Prussia an undertaker, living in the limits of the cemetery, heard during the night the cries proceeding from within the grave in which a person had been buried on the previous day. Not daring to interfere without permission, he went to the police and reported the matter. When, after a great deal of delay, the required formalities were fulfilled and permission granted to open the grave, it was found that the man had been buried alive, but that he was now dead... he had skinned his hand and head in his struggles ...

The narrator in Poe's story arranged a mechanism in the coffin in which he proposed to be buried that would release him on the faintest movement. Tebb and Vellum describe the apparatus invented by Count Karnice-Karnicki, who had once witnessed the premature burial of a Belgian girl. A mechanism in the coffin opened a tube to the outer air and raised a flag above the ground if the supposed corpse showed the slightest sign of life. And then there was the mortuary in Munich, a kind of purgatory for corpses, in which the corpses' fingers were attached for a few days to a bell that rang in an apartment inhabited 24 hours a day by an attendant.

Was any of this necessary? Even now, a person occasionally comes to life at his own postmortem examination. Perhaps I was wiser than I knew when, as an exhausted houseman, a nurse phoned me from the ward in the middle of the night and said, 'Doctor, I think Mr Jones is dead.'

'Well,' I said, 'if you're right, he'll still be dead in the morning,' and went back to sleep.

Drawn to the other side

Poor Sir Oliver Lodge! An eminent physicist, pioneer of radio, competitor with Marconi, he is remembered today, if at all, mainly for having been a propagandist for spiritualism. His best known book, *Raymond or Life and Death*, first published in 1916 and subsequently reprinted many times, recounts his efforts to get in posthumous touch with his son, Raymond, who was killed at Ypres in 1915.

Sir Oliver's pain at losing his son clearly was assuaged by what he thought was evidence of Raymond's continued existence on 'the other side,' and his book, which came with all the authority of a celebrated fellow of the Royal Society, was just what tens of thousands of bereaved parents, for obvious reasons, wanted to read and believe. The book was ridiculed in some circles because Raymond revealed, among other things, that there were still cigars and whiskies and soda in the ethereal realm. In fact, life there continued much as before.

One of the strongest pieces of evidence for Raymond's survival was that his father learnt, through a medium, of the existence of a group photograph taken of Raymond in Belgium just before he died, in which someone leant on his shoulder. Sir Oliver had known nothing of this photograph before, and by coincidence a few days later the mother of a medical officer in Raymond's battalion, who had had it in his possession, sent it to Sir Oliver. The medical officer was Dr Alexander Bruce Cheves, who qualified in Edinburgh in 1911, joined the Royal Army Medical Corps in 1914, and died in 1935. In the photograph, Raymond was sitting in the first row of the group, and the man behind him was leaning on his shoulder.

To us, no doubt, it is surprising that so many brilliant people took spiritualism seriously. Sir William Crookes, the inventor of the cathode tube, and winner of the Nobel prize for physics, was a firm believer. Charles Richet, who won the Nobel prize for medicine in 1913 for his elucidation of anaphylaxis, spent most of the last part of his life writing books with titles such as *The Great Hope*.

But the most famous physician who believed in spiritualism was Sir Arthur Conan Doyle. He had hoped that he would be remembered more for his spiritualist work than for Sherlock Holmes, but it was not to be. In 1918, he wrote a short book called *The New Revelation*, a prelude to his two volume history of spiritualism. Sir Arthur relates the kind of evidence that impressed him:

A lady in whom I was interested had died in a provincial town. She was a chronic invalid, and morphia was found by her bedside. There was an inquest with an open verdict. Eight days later I went to have a sitting with Mr Vout Peters [a favourite medium, incidentally, of Sir Oliver Lodge]. After giving a good deal which was vague and irrelevant, he suddenly said, 'There is a lady here. She is leaning upon an older woman. She keeps saying 'Morphia.' Three times she has said it. Her mind was clouded. She did not mean it. Morphia!' Those were almost his exact words.

Sir Arthur, being a very nice man, could not bring himself to believe in Hell, but he did believe in what he called 'probationary spheres,' for those who had not done well (morally) in life. These, he said, 'should perhaps rather be looked upon as a hospital for weakly souls than as a penal community': a kind of celestial unit for personality disorders, I suppose.

The flaws within

The writer Arthur Machen (1863–1947) wanted to be a doctor but failed at the first hurdle, and his parents were too poor to fund further attempts on his part. Perhaps his thwarted wish to join the profession explains why his stories are so heavily populated by doctors.

Machen wrote tales of the uncanny that enjoyed a considerable vogue in the 1920s and have had their literary admirers, John Betjeman and Jorge Luis Borges among them; but, except by a coterie of devotees, he is largely forgotten now.

The strange thing about Machen's uncanniness is that it exerts its influence largely by physical means. For example, in *The Novel of the White Powder* (hands up all those who did not immediately think of cocaine), Dr Haberden, a general practitioner, writes a prescription for a young man who is studying for the bar and suffering from tiredness caused by overwork. Dr Haberden—there were evidently no problems about confidentiality in those days (that is to say, 1895)—tells his sister:

> *There is nothing really much amiss. No doubt he reads too hard and eats hastily, and then goes back again to his books in too great a hurry, and the natural sequence is some digestive trouble and a little mischief in the nervous system. But I think I do indeed, Miss Leicester—that we shall be able to set this all right. I have written him a prescription which ought to do great things.*

The prescription does indeed do great things. The pharmacist who fills it uses an old powder by mistake that transforms the patient by degrees into 'a dark and putrid mass, seething with corruption and hideous rottenness, neither liquid nor solid,' out of which 'shone two burning points like eyes.' Dr Haberden, seeing what his prescription has done to the patient when he visits him at home, strikes him with an iron bar again and again, in 'the fury of loathing.'

In *The Great God Pan*, published a year earlier, Dr Raymond performs at his home what sounds like a prefrontal leucotomy *avant la letter* on a woman called Mary, who is transformed thereby into a femme fatale who drives all who come in intimate contact with her to suicide.

In *The Terror* it is Dr Lewis, a country practitioner in southwest Wales, who hits upon the explanation of a large series of mysterious and seemingly unconnected deaths. The animals have revolted in concert against the overlordship of mankind: placid dogs turn savagely on their owners, bees sting people to death, sheep drive walkers over cliffs and down quarries, cows trample farmers into marshes, moths form immense clouds that suffocate children to death, and flocks of birds fly into the path of aeroplanes and cause them to crash. The story was written in 1917, when the slaughter of the war deprived humanity of its right to call itself superior to any beings whatsoever.

In so far as Machen is remembered, except by the coterie, it is for originating, by means of a story published in 1914 in the *Evening News*, the myth of the Angel of Mons, according to which bowmen from the Battle of Agincourt were seen protecting the British army from superior German numbers. What started as fiction became accepted fact for a surprising number; apparently it helped the recruitment drive.

In his stories, Machen is unable to decide on the precise relations between the material and immaterial, the physical and the mental—just like us, really.

Too much information

I once read a biography of Somerset Maugham, otherwise excellent, that told me more about his behaviour when demented than I thought I needed—or indeed had any right—to know. Maugham's literary career was over, and revelations about his dementia could hardly cast any useful light on his work. Just because a fact is biographical does not mean that it should appear in a biography.

What, then, of John Bayley's account of the dementia of his wife, Iris Murdoch, the philosopher and novelist? It is often touching and sometimes deeply moving, but at other times it tells me, at least, things I would rather not know. I don't really want to know that an eminent person spent her last years incontinent of urine and with an inclination to put her faeces where they did not belong. I don't want to know that she would have been happy to eat ice cream mixed with baked beans or that at one time Bayley, formerly a professor of English, wanted to hit her. I don't want to know that he shouted 'I really fucking well hate you!' at her.

People less squeamish than I am might say that Bayley here does a public service to those who, with deep devotion and unsung heroism, look after their demented spouses. It would be surprising if many of them did not at times feel anger towards those they have to care for and who are no longer capable of appreciating their sacrifice. To know that a man as educated as Bayley could have been reduced to the above exclamation might bring them comfort.

I suppose the question boils down to whether you think that everything in life should be out in the open or whether some things should remain concealed. I favour the second view, but I think I am now in the minority. It is not merely that, like everyone else (I assume), there are things about me that I would wish no one else to know: I think there are things about everyone I care for that I would not wish to know. The art is in knowing where to draw the line.

The hidden is, in part, what makes life interesting. To say that someone is an open book is also to imply that they are shallow. There are many things that should be skirted over or even brushed under the carpet.

The last two or three decades have seen a vogue for memoirs of illness, by those with the illness and by carers. A magazine once sent me seven such books for review in a single article. The ostensible justification for these books is that they give aid and comfort to people similarly placed; but I do not think this can account for their popularity, because people read about illnesses that they neither have nor are likely ever to have.

I think rather that they are attempts to give meaning to suffering in a post-religious age, to give a transcendent gloss to what otherwise seems arbitrary and unfair. Murdoch's Alzheimer's disease was a terrible affliction, principally for her husband, no doubt: but at least three books and a film came of it.

Peering into the future

Prognosis is, as we all know, an inexact science, at best. Some people live longer than predicted, and some do not survive as long. It is even possible that there have been doctors who, in the secret recesses of their heart, have felt slightly irritated that their patients have defied their crystal clear instructions as to how long to live.

But how accurate would we like prognosis to be? Would any of us like to know in advance the exact time and date of our own death or those of the people around us?

Is all knowledge necessarily good? I once discussed our understanding of the brain with an eminent professor who thought that it was. He was all for maximally increased understanding, whereupon I described a patient of mine who believed that his neighbours had developed an electronic scanner that could read his thoughts at a distance. If such a thing were possible, would it be desirable? I thought not; on the contrary, it would be hell on earth. Only secrecy makes life tolerable.

The science fiction writer Robert A Heinlein (1907-88) wrote a story about perfect prognosis, called 'Life-Line,' first published in 1939. In the story a maverick researcher called Pinero, of indeterminate scientific discipline and the provenance of whose doctorate is questioned by orthodox scientists who don't want to believe him, has developed a machine that is able to predict with great accuracy the time and date of any person's death.

At a meeting of the Academy of Science Dr Pinero is insulted and shouted down. A doctor in the audience objects that if a man is apprised of his time of death he might very well die at that time as a self fulfilling prophecy, for psychological reasons, 'whether the distinguished speaker's mechanical egg-timer works or not.'

Dr Pinero suggests an experiment to overcome this objection. Life insurance companies try to obtain an injunction against the experiment, because if Pinero's device worked it would completely destroy the need for or indeed possibility of life insurance. Dr Pinero replies that he is only doing retail what the actuaries of life insurance companies do wholesale.

He, or rather his machine, correctly predicts the time of his death, very near in the future: he is murdered at the behest of the chief of a life insurance company, and his machine, whose secret he has not divulged, is smashed beyond repair by vandals in the pay of the company.

For myself I side with the vandals, having always had a secret sympathy with the Luddites. A fortune teller at a funfair once predicted when I was 16 that I should live to be 84, and since her only other two predictions (that I should be a doctor and travel extensively) have come to pass I cannot help but wonder whether I shall spend the 84th year of my age in a state of anxiety, notwith-standing the scientific absurdity of her proceedings. Fortunately she kept her predictions to three because I paid her only half a crown instead of five shillings. For the higher sum I probably would have learnt the nature of my last illness and would have been turned into a hypochondriacal wreck.

Heinlein made many prescient predictions or guesses. Among the least happy, written in 1949, is: 'There are still more outhouse than flush toilets in the United States, the land of inside plumbing. And the ratio will not have changed very much on the day when men first walk the silent face of the Moon.'

Vorsprung durch technik?

Many doctors have been famous writers, many famous writers had a medical parent, and many doctors appear as characters in novels and plays: but this is not enough to establish a special connection between medicine and literature, at least for those pedants who will not countenance a statement without the strongest possible evidence in its favour. Before a connection can be honestly asserted, our pedant will say, we need to know that there have been more doctors who were writers, more writers with a medical parent, and more doctors as characters in literature than could be expected by chance.

There are obviously problems here with both numerator and denominator. Who is to count as a writer? Any doctor who has published a book in any literary form or on any literary subject? Even more difficult is the question of who doctors are properly to be compared with. The whole of humanity? Bricklayers? Fishmongers? Lawyers? These difficulties notwithstanding, I am convinced that the connection between medicine and literature is and has been a real one. But will it survive?

In the past, the connection between medicine and literature was spontaneous or natural, arising from the general education that all doctors had received, combined with their experience of human existence, an experience that was necessarily wider, deeper, and more varied than that of most people. Doctors are privy, after all, to their patients' deepest secrets, but at the same time retain an attitude of objectivity. No situation could be more propitious for a writer.

However, with the increasing technical demands made upon medical students, it is possible that they are more narrowly educated than their predecessors were. Some medical schools now attempt to remedy this putative narrowness by teaching medical humanities as part of the course. But the spontaneous link between medicine and literature has been broken.

Does this matter? Is there any evidence that broadly educated doctors are better doctors precisely because of the breadth of their education? I suspect that there is not. In any case, it is clear that high artistic and literary cultivation does not by itself necessarily translate into fine moral qualities. For example, in his famous wartime memoir *Kaputt*, the Italian journalist and writer Curzio Malaparte describes a man who speaks perfect Italian though it is not his native tongue; discourses learnedly on Plato and Marsilio Ficino; has spent days and days studying the paintings in the Pitti Palace and the Uffizi; loves Chopin and Brahms; and plays the piano 'divinely.' This man is none other than Hans Frank, head of the general government of Poland at a time when some of the worst atrocities in the history of the world were committed there, a man in short who was among the very worst of the very worst. His intellectual and aesthetic refinement did not prevent him from believing that the Führer's will was the highest source of law or from seeing nothing wrong with the mass extermination of his fellow beings.

Furthermore, there is no reason why a doctor should not be highly accomplished in a severely technical discipline without being cultivated in any other sense. A doctor who can discourse beautifully on the sonnets of Shakespeare but who cannot operate is no use to someone with a surgical condition. And because medicine seems destined to become ever more technical, with knowledge and technical procedures increasing exponentially, there is no reason to suppose that our eminent doctors of the future either can or ought to be like eminent figures of the past, such as Geoffrey Keynes and Russell Brain, who were able to straddle the two worlds with almost equal distinction.

For all this, I cannot rid myself entirely of the idea that doctors should be broadly educated. The time is surely still far in the future when doctors will have to be technicians and nothing else; and it does not follow from the fact that not every doctor needs to be broadly educated that no doctor does, any more than it follows from the fact that not every doctor needs to know intimately the biochemistry of hepatolenticular degeneration means that no doctor does. Yet I remain bothered by the still small voice of my inner pedant, who demands evidence that even in the non-technical sphere of medicine the broadly educated doctor is better than the narrowly educated one.

Perhaps things should be approached differently. Let us grant for a moment that it is not necessary for a doctor to be broadly educated or cultivated in any way. If it is true of doctors, it is likely to be true of every other group you can think of: lawyers, accountants, teachers, engineers, and so forth. In other words, there is no need for anyone to be broadly educated or cultivated.

But if no one is broadly educated or cultivated, that is the end of broad education and cultivation itself. We will be reduced to a society of technocrats, each absorbed in their own narrow specialism. Notwithstanding the horrible example of Hans Frank, this is not a state of society to which I look forward. Apart from anything else, some among us will be specialists in the exercise of power, against whom the rest of us will be defenceless.

Enslaved to credulity

The persistence of charlatanry irritates doctors, who would much prefer to have a monopoly of foolishness as well as of wisdom. How is it that those who strain at the gnats of science so often swallow the camels of superstition?

Dr Verdo, from the town of Marmande in the Lot and Garonne, set out in 1867 to answer this question in his short book *Charlatanry and Charlatans in Medicine: A Psychological Study*. He classified firstly the consumers and then the producers of charlatanry, using his own experience and intuition rather than the methods favoured today. This conduced to brevity, if not necessarily to accuracy.

Dr Verdo says that women are in first place of those susceptible to the lure of charlatans and their wares, for women are 'impression-able, changeable and tender, and judge more by imagination and feeling than by logic and good sense.' Next come artists and mystic poets, 'sensitive souls who are a little mad, and float above the realities of life, searching for unknown shores beyond inhabited regions.'

After them are the gamblers, soldiers, sailors, industrialists, and speculators—all those who habitually take risks. Peasants are next, whose ignorance and isolation predisposes to superstition. The least susceptible to charlatanry are doctors, philosophers, physicists, and other scientists who are 'used to examining the causes of things, to sound out the secrets of nature, and are always wary of the errors of judgment that could lead them to think the supernatural at work.' But even they may fear Fridays and 13 at table.

Dr Verdo divides charlatans into two classes: the public charlatan and the charlatan in private practice. The public charlatan cries his wares to all and sundry, dresses flashily, and claims to have received the secret of his panacea somewhere in the mystic orient. (I have a wonderful French print from the middle of the 19th century of a man addressing a credulous crowd, claiming to have been the king of Persia's physician and who offers his balm to the crowd only because it cured everyone in Persia and there was nothing left for him to do there.)

The charlatan in private practice, by contrast, is a self proclaimed specialist, for example in gout or in 'an illness of adventurers that I do not want to name' (and that, in our franker age, was once treated in the 'special clinic'). Unlike the public charlatan, who revels in the light of day, the charlatan in private practice is a creature of ill-lit rooms, decorated in cheap luxury.

Dr Verdo is a realist; he knows that charlatans flourish wherever real doctors have failed, for example in 'cancer, scrofula, phthisis, tetanus, croup, whooping cough, gout, rabies, migraine, sea-sickness, epilepsy, rheumatism, asthma, cholera, etc.' This list perhaps explains why a friend of Dr Verdo's, who was a student with him, gave up medicine for economic reasons and took up lucrative charlatanry.

But for Dr Verdo there is a deeper reason why charlatanry and charlatans always flourish. He begins his book with the words, 'The inclination to the marvellous is in human nature itself,' and he ends his book with the words, 'Credulity is one of the attributes that distinguishes man from the animals.'

I think this is true because while we fear the unknown we fear the known almost as much, and thus we fly for relief from the one to the other.

Attitude to method

There was a time when medical history was written as the story of the gradual ascent of knowledge to our glorious present; this was known as the Whig interpretation of history. Obviously it had its limitations (it was mainly written by retired doctors), but it turns out that all other interpretations have their limitations too.

In his amusing book *Quacks: Fakers and Charlatans in English Medicine*, the non-medical medical historian Roy Porter consistently minimises the difference between what in the 18th century was called 'the faculty' (that is to say the regular practitioners armed with a *bona fide* medical degree) and the irregulars: the mountebanks and the charlatans. After all, says Porter, is there evidence that the treatment of the faculty was more effective than that of the quacks? Near the end of the book he writes, 'There was far greater convergence between the activities and attitudes of regulars and quacks than either side allowed, or than historians have been primed to perceive.'

Well, yes and no. As it happened I read John Huxham in tandem with Porter. Huxham (1692–1768) was a regular physician who discovered nothing, in the sense that there is no Huxham's disease, Huxham's law, or Huxham's sign; it can even be said that he missed a golden opportunity to discover the cause of an epidemic. Yet, though he discovered nothing, and his results with his patients were probably little better than those of the veriest mountebank, yet when one reads him one cannot but respect the diligence, rationality, and devotion with which he investigated the causes of epidemics.

Huxham was a Devon man who studied at Leiden and received his degree from Rheims. He returned to England to practise at Plymouth; in his *Observations on the Air and Epidemic Diseases: from the year MDCCXXVIII to MDCCXXXVII Inclusive* one finds an immense accumulation of meteorological data, which he tries to relate to the prevalence of epidemic diseases. January 1728, for example, was 'a very rainy, moist Season, for in this Month fell no less than 6 inches, of Rain, an immense Quantity!' The state of public health was as follows:

> *From the Beginning of the Month Coughs and Catarrhs were frequent, oftentimes attended with a troublesome Tumor of the Fauces, and slight Fevers commonly. Rheumatisms and Squinzies up and down; great lowness of spirits and frequent hysteric Paroxysms every-where.*

We may smile at the naivety of this, but it is a serious, if unsuccessful, attempt to interrogate nature by a rational method completely different from that of, say, an itinerant seller of nostrums. So it's not surprising that, *pace* Porter's faintly disguised sneers, progress depended upon the faculty and not upon the quacks.

Huxham's missed opportunity came in 1724. Fourteen years later he published *A Small Treatise on the Devonshire Colic which Was very Epidemic in the Year MDCCXXIV*. He described how, in the cider season, many people were seized with intestinal colic, palsies of their arms and hands, peripheral anaesthesia, and unconsciousness and seizures from which they died. He attributed this to the acid in the apples rather than to the lead of the vats in which the cider was kept.

That the long continued Use, shall I say? Or Abuse of this Apple Drink was the Cause of this Disease I doubt not, for I saw no one seized with it, that abstained... Nor did it attack people of the better Sort, who lived elegantly, for they despising cheap Things, scarce ever tasted the Apples...

It was Sir George Baker (1722–1809) who, during the height of Georgian quackery, proved that it was the lead in the vats that did it.

A form of truth

It is a melancholy reflection (but also a testimony to the fact of more recent progress) that the question of whether the ancients or moderns were best was a live one in the first half of the 18th century, with regard not only to literature, where progress is perhaps rather difficult to assess or measure, but also to medicine, where progress is rather less difficult to recognise.

Francis Clifton, who had a medical degree from Leiden and was physician to the Prince of Wales, wrote his book *The State of Physick, Ancient and Modern, Briefly Consider'd: With a Plan for the Improvement of It* in 1732. He had no doubts on the matter: the ancients, particularly Hippocrates, were superior to the moderns. This was largely because they observed better and treated less.

The superiority of Hippocrates' knowledge of diseases was made manifest in the superiority of his prognoses; and prognostication was, in Clifton's opinion, the second most important task of the physician after cure. But further research was needed, because not all diseases had been known to him, and here Clifton lists a few, with their origins, that had not yet appeared in the ancient world: 'the Small-pox, for instance, from the Arabians; the Venereal disease from the Spaniards; the Scurvy from the Portuguese; and the Rickets from our own country.'

The scurvy introduced and spread by the Portuguese? This seems a little odd at first sight; but assuming that Clifton's scurvy was vitamin C deficiency, there is an explanation. The Portuguese were the first oceangoing sailors and therefore the first, presumably, to suffer shipboard scurvy en masse. It would be as reasonable to suspect that they had transmitted it to the rest of Europe afterwards as that the Spanish had brought syphilis from the Americas.

For Clifton, then, the task was for the moderns to catch up with Hippocrates. He granted that the modern 'materia medica' was superior to the ancient, with many more preparations, but unfortunately some of it was dangerous when injudiciously used, and it was a moot point whether modern physicians killed or cured more. At least Hippocrates refrained from killing.

Dr Clifton's plan for the improvement of the practice of physick was simple: it was that more Baconian observation should be undertaken. He suggested that every public hospital should have three or four people in the IT department, the IT in question being a form to be filled in every day about every patient (in Greek and Latin), with such matters as the weather conditions and the prevailing direction of the wind, the patient's clinical condition, the response to treatment, and the eventual outcome. The three or four people would, of course, be completely independent of the physicians and surgeons treating patients, so that the information would not be biased.

From the great mass of information gathered, it was hoped—no, expected—that valuable knowledge would result as to the proper classification of diseases, their causes, their prognosis, and their proper treatment. In other words, if only enough information were gathered by enough people using enough forms, valuable truth would emerge spontaneously, like the birth of Venus. Does this, by any chance, sound familiar? Who, indeed, were better: the ancients or the moderns?

Define progress

It is difficult not to write the history of medicine as the history of progress; but how is progress measured, and when exactly did it begin? Discoveries were often made a very long time before anyone benefited from them. Is progress an increase in knowledge, in curative power, or in both? When was the first life saved by the anatomy of Vesalius?

These questions came to my mind as I was reading Ibn al-Jazzar on fevers. Ibn al-Jazzar was an eminent physician of the 10th century who practised in North Africa and wrote a compendium of medicine, *Provisions for the Traveller and Nourishment for the Sedentary*, that was famous in its day and was translated into Latin and Greek. It was used in the first Western medical school of Salerno, and I read the chapters (duly translated, I hasten to add) that came from it.

A commonplace of medical history is that, at the time, Arabic medicine was far in advance of that of Western Europe. Judging from Ibn al-Jazzar on fevers, it is not easy to make sense of this claim. It is not, of course, that medicine in Western Europe was advanced—very far from it. The conditions of life in Europe at that time were primitive and appalling. Life for most people was probably nasty, brutish, and short. But al-Jazzar displays no knowledge of the causes of fever, nor is it likely that any of his proposed remedies actually cured anyone. Without either knowledge or therapeutic efficacy, it is difficult for us to understand how his system of medicine can have been more advanced than any other at the time, unless the other was more positively harmful than his.

Furthermore, he did not seem to understand the need to provide any evidence for what he said, except by reference to Galen as an unimpeachable authority. This is not to blame him: he was a man of his time and place, and we who believe in evidence based medicine would have been exactly as he was if we had been of his time and place.

When he tells us that what he calls ardent fever is caused by 'the sharp, fiery, yellow bile that has collected in the cavities of the veins that are adjacent to the heart' and that anyone who has the fever should be administered 'juice of tamarind, plums, and jujube with the core of reedy Indian laburnum, manna from Khurasan, preserved violets, a drink made from plums and the like,' it is evident that we are a mental universe away from ourselves.

Yet it is true that al-Jazzar would be preferred to what was on offer in Western Europe at the time. Al-Jazzar believed in cleanliness, for example, and therefore in bathing, often in water infused with pleasant smelling flowers and herbs. This would surely have been soothing, though not curative. And his prescriptions are not obviously repellent (as so many Western prescriptions were to remain for many centuries to come), consisting mainly of cool drinks and perfumed syrups. They imply a high general level of refinement.

But is this enough to call his medical system advanced? It is far better to soothe than to cause additional discomfort, of course, but that cannot be the principal aim of medicine. It is only with the self conscious, disciplined, and systematic search for truth that medical progress can be said to have begun.

Civility

The lot of secondhand booksellers is not a happy one. The trade has nearly gone the way of cooperage or farriery. Customers are growing older and are not being replaced when they die; but many booksellers cannot retire as they would like, because their stock remains unsold. On the contrary it grows as they buy more books than they sell. They know, therefore, that they will die in harness, among the mould, the dust, and the silverfish that inhabit the drier parts of their establishments.

The other day I bought a book from a bookseller for £4. He was delighted, almost triumphant. 'I knew I would sell it one day,' he said, adding: 'To the right purchaser.' He spoke as if the book were a puppy that needed a good home. 'It's been on the shelf for 10 years, but I always knew someone would buy it in the end.'

What was the title that so vindicated his acumen? It was *The White Women's Protection Ordinance: Sexual Anxiety and Politics in Papua*, a subject of extreme specialist interest, I should imagine, by Amirah Inglis. (As I tell booksellers who mark their books 'rare,' purchasers are even rarer.) But I have long believed that enlightenment is to be sought in the most obscure places.

Extremely well written, this book recounts the agitation in Port Moresby in the 1920s for the protection of Australian women from the sexual advances of the Papuans, who, as primitive men, were thought to have but poor control over their impulses. (Papua was then a territory ruled by Australia.)

The white population was very small, and as writers such as Somerset Maugham, Stefan Zweig, and Graham Greene realised, such communities were like cultures of human nature in a Petri dish. Passions were easily inflamed.

The author relates how a new doctor, one Mathews by name, arrived in Port Moresby and quickly became a favourite of the women, who preferred him to the doctors already there.

He fell foul of the establishment, however, and was barred from treating private patients in the government hospital. When a nun, Sister Pascal, went down with malaria, she insisted on none other than Mathews as her doctor, and his partisans had a belligerent confrontation at the hospital with special constables sworn in to prevent him from entering. The establishment won: soon afterwards Dr Mathews returned whence he had come.

The ordinance of the book's title provided for the death penalty for rape or attempted rape and for flogging up to three times, 50 strokes each, for lesser offences. Among the members of the territory's unelected legislative council was the chief medical officer, Dr W M Strong, who was also the government anthropologist. He moved unsuccessfully in the council to get the penalty for attempted rape reduced from death. He then tried unsuccessfully to move a reduction in the number of floggings and the number of strokes per flogging for lesser offences. His final ploy was to move that floggings ought to be in public, knowing that if the council accepted this proposal the whole ordinance, which he opposed, would be thrown out by the Australian government.

His final speech was a little gem of irony:

When [Papua] was an uncivilized country these punishments were not needed. The civilization we have introduced has resulted in the country becoming so uncivilized that we have to inflict punishment that we would not have done when it was not at all civilized.

Permission to lie?

In his letter to Consentius, the 5th-century Gallic grammarian, on the subject of lying, St Augustine discussed the question of whether it would be permissible to conceal from a very ill man that his son had died, if it was thought that the truth would harm him. Although Augustine sympathised with the motive for the lie, he held that it was impermissible to tell it, for two reasons: because it was against scripture to lie, and because once lying for good causes was permissible it would soon spread and make trustful human communication more difficult.

The philosopher Sissela Bok generally takes more or less the same line, though without the scriptural apparatus or justification. Her book about lying is called *Lying: Moral Choice in Public and Private Life*, and it is either annoying or sobering, depending on your point of view, that there are more references to the medical profession in the index than to lawyers, politicians, and secondhand car salesmen combined. Am I paranoid, or is there a lot of ill informed prejudice against doctors?

Bok's book was first published in 1978, when doctors were no doubt much more paternalistic towards their patients than they are now. Nevertheless, I find the singling out of the medical profession in a book about lying—how can I put it delicately?—unrealistic.

As an example of paternalistic lying the philosopher gives the case of a mother who said that she wished to donate her kidney to her daughter, who needed a transplant. Unfortunately, whenever the donation was about to be made, the mother fell ill with psychosomatic symptoms, until the doctors concluded that subconsciously she did not really want to make the donation. In the end, they told her that they had discovered that she was not a suitable donor, disguising from her the real reason why they declined to proceed.

Was this lie justified? Would it have been better to confront the mother with her subconscious reluctance? The answer to this question surely depends on whether or not the mother's suffering consequent upon the revelation of her reluctance could be overcome and replaced by an equable acceptance of the truth. The doctors, presumably, thought that it could not, and therefore that it was kinder to lie.

Bok concedes that paternalism is not always and in every case wrong. But if paternalism is not always wrong, then there must be an ethical principle morally anterior to, or higher than, the right to patient autonomy: for first must come the doctor's decision whether the case before him is one in which his duty to be paternalistic overrides the patient's right to autonomy.

These are difficult questions over which philosophers have wrestled, without coming to any indisputable conclusion, for millennia. I remember how, once, all fired up by the relatively new first principle of patient autonomy, I explained to a patient the statistical logic of antihypertensives: how the chances were that they would do him no good, but how, if they did do him good, it would be a very great good. Then, at the end of my little disquisition, I asked him whether he wanted to take the pills or not.

'I don't know,' he said. 'You're the doctor.'

8. Sic transit

The father of cremation

In his wonderful memoir of his early life in the Rhondda Valley and in London, *Print of a Hare's Foot*, Rhys Davies (1901-78) devotes an entire chapter to Dr William Price of Llantrisant. Dr Price (1800-93) was eccentric, to put it mildly; but he was a real doctor, having qualified in 1821 at Barts in record time. He is said to have cured many where others failed; he operated surgically only as a last resort or (by his own admission) if he needed the money.

Davies's memoirs lend romance to a time and place that, superficially at least, rather lack it if one just looks at old photographs. Davies was born in relatively privileged circumstances, being the son of the founder and owner of the Royal Stores of Clydach Vale. He devotes eloquent paragraphs to the prickly Welsh flannel shirt that he was made to wear, which served a dual spiritual and physical purpose, the discomfort being good for the soul and the material itself being thought to ward off chest infections. Another way to prevent such infections was to stick a child's head out of the railway carriage window as the train went through a tunnel, a method of prophylaxis available, of course, only to the better off.

The chapter on Dr Price appears in the book because his memory loomed large in the Welsh valleys at the time, and Davies's mother and grandmother remembered him well. Most of Davies's information, however, seems to have come from a pamphlet first published in 1940 by Thomas Islwyn ap Nicholas, *A Welsh Heretic: Dr William Price, Llantrisant*. Islwyn ap Nicholas was an Aberystwyth dentist who wrote several pamphlets about Welsh radicals, but that is all I have been able to discover about him. Unlike doctors, dentists do not take easily to the pen; as to their political views I am ill informed, but I suspect that few of them are sympathetic to radicalism.

Dr Price of Llantrisant (where there is now a statue of him) fell foul of the law on several occasions. He supported a Chartist (worker) uprising and had to flee to France for a time. But in effect he was a born oppositionist.

From an early age he sunbathed naked on Welsh hillsides (when there was sun), which did not endear him to the preachers of the local chapels. He believed himself to be a druid, wrote in an archaic Welsh all his own, and wore red trousers, a green tunic, and a complete fox skin on his head. He grew a long white beard and refused to wear socks. He was a vegetarian, claiming that to eat the flesh of animals was to take on their characteristics (exactly what a vegetarian cousin of mine claimed a century later), and was an anti-vaccinationist. He was in favour of free love and fathered a child at the age of 87.

He was the father of British cremation, believing burial to be unhygienic and wasteful. In 1884 he tried to cremate his 5 month old son (called Jesus Christ Price) but was arrested in the attempt. A howling mob attacked his home for his blasphemy, but at his trial— Dr Price always defended himself—he was acquitted by the judge, James Fitzjames Stephen, author of the classic riposte to John Stuart Mill's *On Liberty* and uncle of Virginia Woolf. Henceforth cremation was permissible under UK law.

The howling mob changed its mind too. Around 20,000 people attended Dr Price's own cremation, nine years later.

Today's stars

Even eminent people are soon forgotten, and I don't suppose that the name of Sir John Collie (1862-1935) will mean much to most readers, even though he was knighted twice, first for his medical services to the Metropolitan Water Board, and second for his medical services during the First World War.

The nature of his researches can perhaps best be grasped from the titles of a few of his books: *Fraud and its Detection in Accident Insurance Cases* (1912), *Malingering and Feigned Sickness* (1913—dedicated to 'my friend the British Workman to whom I owe much'), and *Fraud in Medico-Legal Practice* (1932).

His obituary was not such as one might wish for oneself. Although he was really very kind, said the obituarist, some people sent to him for examination were so frightened that they were left almost paralysed, if not by the industrial accident that had brought them there, then by the prospect of the encounter.

The trouble is, of course, that fraud and malingering really do exist, and unless they be counted as diseases in themselves a doctor sometimes has to pass judgment on them. Collie's book, *Medico-legal Examinations and the Workmen's Compensation Act, 1906* (1912) elaborates on this at some length, in an excellent prose style.

That the prospect of compensation can play tricks on the human mind is surely within the experience of many doctors. Collie says:

> *Many a workman who would scorn to rob his employer of a penny is induced by the working of this Act to formulate an inflated, if not an unjust, claim for compensation… many of the abuses are the result of petty intrigues, and he is but the tool of unscrupulous agents…*

In short, of lawyers: for if you ask *cui bono*, the answer is obvious: 'Several times working men have appealed to me, saying in effect that whilst the lawyers fight they starve.'

Some of Sir John's methods of uncovering fraud would perhaps not find approval today. In those days, it was a common or urban myth that low back injury caused insensibility of the skin over the area of the injury, and in one case Sir John, who suspected the man of malingering, applied his electric battery to the man's back.

'I applied the battery. The claimant said he did not feel it over the painful area. I made the current considerably stronger, and he tried to bear it manfully. At last, with a howl, he fell in a heap on the ground. I told him to get up and not make a fool of himself.'

The story, though, has a happy ending.

> *His wife, hearing the yell, came into the room, and I explained to her that I*

had cured him with the battery. I said I was very pleased; he said he was; and the wife agreed with both of us. He said he would go back to work forthwith, and he did so.

My copy of this book was inscribed by Sir John to none other than Lloyd George, the most important member of the government that passed the Workmen's Compensation Act. My copy of Sir John's *Fraud in Medico-Legal Practice* once belonged to Sydney Dernley, who was the last surviving hangman (or should it be hangperson?) of England.

A telling tale

For half a century the Indian author R K Narayan chronicled the everyday life of his fictional town of Malgudi, in reality his home town of Mysore. He had that ability to see (and convey in words) a universe in a grain of sand that is, perhaps, the mark of a great writer.

The protagonist of his short story 'The Doctor's Word,' published in 1947 in the collection *The Astrologer's Day*, is Dr Raman. He is a specialist of sorts: people go or are brought to him only as a last resort. This causes Dr Raman to demand why they did not come to him earlier, exactly the question I used peevishly to ask in a tropical country where I once worked when people were brought to me with paraplegia caused by Pott's disease of the spine. The answer was that it was only then that they lost faith in the power of magic to effect a cure.

Dr Raman is respected, however, because of his plain speaking: 'He was not a mere doctor expressing an opinion but a judge pronouncing a verdict.' He tells patients when they are dying because 'he never believed that agreeable words ever saved lives.'

His principle of plain speaking is sorely tested, however, when he is called to the bedside of one of his closest friends, Gopal, who is dangerously ill. On asking why he was not called earlier, he receives the reply, 'We thought you would be busy and did not wish to trouble you unnecessarily'—precisely the answer I received 30 years later as a locum general practitioner when called to the bedside of an 80 year old man who had become severely anaemic from chronic rectal bleeding.

Dr Raman operates on Gopal but without expectation of success. Gopal wakes after the operation and asks Dr Raman whether he will survive. Dr Raman finds himself unable to return a straight answer and prevaricates. Gopal then asks him to witness his will, because if he dies intestate the circling human vultures will rob his widow of his rightful estate; and he knows that if Dr Raman agrees to witness the will it means that he believes that he, Gopal, will die.

Gopal is weak and sleepy after the operation.

'Dr Raman called, 'Gopal, listen.' This was the first time he was going to do a piece of acting before a patient, simulate a feeling, and conceal his judgment.

'He stooped over the patient and said with deliberate emphasis, 'Don't worry about the will now. You are going to live.' The patient asked in a tone of relief, 'Do you say so? If it comes from your lips, it must be true...''

Shortly afterwards Dr Raman gives his assistant instructions to ease Gopal's passing with an injection if the expected death struggle becomes too painful. But in fact Gopal does not die, and the next day Dr Raman says to his assistant, 'How he has survived will be a puzzle to me all my life.'

Only six and a half pages long, it seems to me that 'The Doctor's Word' might serve as a useful starting point for the teaching of medical ethics, for medical practice is to medical ethics what literature is to philosophy.

The bill for bloodletting

There has long been a controversy over how the name M'Naghten, of the so called M'Naghten Rules, or criteria for legal insanity, should be spelt. Richard Moran, in his 1981 book on the case, *Knowing Right from Wrong,* says that there are 12 known spellings; he plumps for McNaughtan.

This, of course, is not the only controversy surrounding it. M'Naghten shot Edward Drummond, Sir Robert Peel's private secretary, in 1843, mistaking him for the prime minister himself.

(Oddly enough, Professor Moran adds to the confusion by being unable to decide whether the victim was called Edward or Edmund Drummond.) M'Naghten believed that he was being persecuted by the government and the Tory party and was found not guilty by reason of insanity. The public was outraged by this apparent leniency, regarding it as an invitation to assassination, and judges were asked to pronounce on what constituted insanity of a degree that absolved a man from criminal responsibility.

There was yet another controversy about the case, started by a doctor called Samuel Dickson. He wrote an incendiary pamphlet, published in the year of the murder, titled *What Killed Mr Drummond, the Lead or the Lancet?*

Dickson (1802-69) was a ferocious opponent of the practice of bloodletting with a lancet. He is scathing about the medical treatment of Drummond, who did not die until five days after he was shot:

> *The ball was extracted on the evening of the wound. Why this hurry to extract the ball? The unfortunate gentleman is already wounded, and a new wound must needs be made at a time like this, to extract a ball that was perfectly passive; to say nothing of the previous groping for the ball, after enlarging its point of entrance—the last place in the world where it could possibly be expected to be found! Did the unfortunate patient suffer no corporeal or mental agony while all was doing?*

Drummond was shot just before the discovery of anaesthesia, and so agony was surely not too strong a word. But worse was to follow:

> *What might have been expected—Fever—And what was the Treatment?—Blood-letting repeated and re-repeated—twice in One day!—leeches in numbers were also applied and bleeding AGAIN resorted to. The temporal artery was in the first instance opened! and the result of all—DEATH!*

Dickson believed that without this treatment Drummond would have survived. Dickson was a violent critic of the medical orthodoxy of his day, having been an army surgeon in India where he noticed that bloodletting, which he then applied uncritically to patients with dysentery, malaria, and cholera, usually ended in death. In his *Report on the Endemic Cholera* of 1829, *The Fallacy of the Art of Physic* of 1836, and *Fallacies of the Faculty* of 1839, he accused his fellow practitioners of ignorance, illogicality, and a desire to prolong illnesses in their avidity for the fees with which bloodletting provided them. Among other things he suggested a controlled trial for the efficacy of bleeding in pneumonia.

His own method of treating fever—an emetic, quinine, and cold water splashed on the body—with which he wanted to compare bloodletting was probably less dangerous. But as bloodletting declined as a practice, Dickson received no thanks and even less praise for having pointed out its dangers. He became ever more bitter, criticising in print all the leaders of the profession. His obituary in the *Medical Times and Gazette* said that he was a man of moderate ability with 'a talent for abuse which he exercised to an unlimited extent.' But his worst offence by far was that of having been right.

An author spurned

Almost everyone who has written for publication has received letters of rejection; and I think it a fair surmise that almost everyone reacts, at least in the first instance, by supposing that the fault lies not with what they have written but with the blindness and folly of the publisher.

This was certainly the reaction of H Charlton Bastian (1837-1915)—emeritus professor of the principles and practice of medicine at University College London and physician to the National Hospital in Queen Square—to the refusal of the Royal Society (of which he was a fellow) to publish his researches into the spontaneous generation of bacteria.

In the foreword to his book *The Origin of Life: Being an Account of Experiments with Certain Superheated Saline Solutions in Hermetically Sealed Vessels*, published in 1911, he writes with all the anger of the prophet (or crank) unheard and the author spurned: 'What is the object of the Society but to advance Natural Knowledge? And how can it expect to do this if it tries to stifle or ignore that which is adverse to generally accepted beliefs?'

Bastian was a distinguished neurologist whose researches and publications on aphasia are regarded as classics in their field. (He was also an erudite naturalist, discovering 100 new species of nematode worm.) But his real life's work, in his own opinion, was his research into the origins of life itself. He was an early believer in the theory of evolution, but he pointed out that, logically speaking, life must have had an origin; and he went on to conclude that there was no reason why, if it had originated once, it should not have continued to originate. In defiance of Pasteur and other luminaries he set out to demonstrate that this was so.

He resigned from his chair at University College in 1898 to pursue his private researches. He put a mixture of distilled water, sodium silicate, ammonium phosphate, phosphoric acid, and pernitrate of iron in glass flasks, sealed them, heated them to 130°C, exposed them to the sunlight, and opened them after varying lengths of time, whereupon he found that torulae, bacilli, cocci and penicillium-like moulds had developed in the flask. He hypothesised that silicon had taken the place of carbon in these organisms.

His findings were not accepted, to say the least. He also held other eccentric views, such as heterogenesis: the belief that bacteria do not always reproduce themselves but sometimes emerge as amoebae, ciliated protozoa, and so on. He also believed that bacteria might originate in the cells of multicellular organisms, a view that gave comfort to those who argued that germs did not cause disease: rather, disease caused germs.

His books, finding no favour elsewhere, were published by Watts and Co, which founded the Rationalist Press Association and published titles such as *Humanity's Gain from Unbelief* by Charles Bradlaugh (the first militantly atheist member of parliament, who would stride on to the stage at public meetings, take out his pocket watch, and challenge God to strike him dead within a minute).

Bastian as good as accused the Royal Society of hypocrisy. He quoted against it the statement at the beginning of the volumes of its *Transactions*:

The grounds of [the Society's] choice are, and will continue to be, the importance and singularity of the subjects, or the advantageous manner of treating them, without pretending to answer for the certainty of the facts, or propriety of the reasoning, which must still rest on the judgment of the respective authors.

Odium theologicum (theological hatred) is by no means confined to theologians.

Mortality and immortality

The Prix Goncourt, whose British equivalent is the Booker prize, was won in 2001 by a doctor, Jean-Christophe Rufin, for his historical novel *Rouge Brésil*. The author has had a remarkable career; he is what the French call a *surdoué*—a prodigy.

An early member of Médecins Sans Frontières, Rufin has worked in Africa, Latin America, and Asia. A consultant in neurology in Paris, he has also been French cultural attaché in Brazil and French ambassador to Senegal. He has fulfilled many administrative and academic duties, learnt several languages, and written 15 books, translated into many tongues, that have sold millions of copies worldwide. He became an *immortel*, one of the 40 members of the Académie Française, in 2008.

This year he published a book of short stories: *Sept histoires qui reviennent de loin* (*Seven Stories from Afar*). One of them is called 'Night on Duty,' which I suspect is autobiographical, although Rufin in an interview once put the role of memory in the work of imaginative writing rather beautifully: it is not the writing of memories, but of echoes of memories.

In the story, the narrator is a young doctor aged 24, on duty and dog tired, having been woken many times in the night. Trying to get some sleep in the on-call room, he is woken by a nurse who slides a death certificate under the door for him to sign without going to the trouble of seeing the patient. He begins to sign it and then is seized by conscience; he goes to the ward where the man has died.

In Rufin's story, which takes place in 1975, the man who died had been in a ward for incurables for 12 years. Although to someone of my age 1975 does not seem so very long ago, the conditions in the public hospital that Rufin describes seem medieval from today's standpoint: iron beds crowded together in a long ward, where your neighbour in the next bed 'means a smile and conversation, but also spittle and urine,' and where screens placed around a bed signify death or its approach.

The narrator is very young, inexperienced, and uncertain of himself; the nurses who watch him as he approaches the dead man are infinitely more experienced than he. But the law has conferred upon him the exclusive right to pronounce a man dead, and he trembles as he approaches the dead man: 'Death in France does not have a clear definition. The law prescribes means of authenticating it: longitudinal arteriotomy is the most certain.'

The absence of pulsatile blood is supposedly diagnostic; but the narrator chooses the absence of the corneal reflex instead. He puts the pulp of his thumb on the dead man's open eye.

It takes him a long time to rid his hands of 'the tenacious and imperceptible smell of dead eyes. Today, more than twenty years later, I can still smell it.' For me, it is the smell of the dissecting room that my mind's nose can conjure at will, and sometimes involuntarily.

What use a doctor?

Once upon a time, and quite unlike in our own days, eminence in the medical profession was not entirely dependent on merit, if by merit we mean only intellectual or scientific distinction. A good illustration of this is the career of Sir George Clark (1788-1870), physician to Queen Victoria. He was famous in his day, but he discovered nothing.

His career was interesting. He was the son of the butler to the Earl of Findlater. He qualified as a naval surgeon and was shipwrecked twice. He then studied in Paris and was one of the first British physicians to use the newfangled stethoscope. He then practised in Rome, living near the Piazza di Spagna. There he treated John Keats for four months, failing to diagnose the dying poet's tuberculosis, notwithstanding his stethoscope—or, as some say, failing to tell him the diagnosis from a kindly wish to spare his feelings.

Then he returned to Britain and became a fashionable physician, treating Prince Albert and failing to diagnose his fatal typhoid (not that it would have made any difference if he had).

Clark was also physician to the philosopher John Stuart Mill. The first time Mill consulted him was after he had been given a plaster impregnated with belladonna to treat a twisted ankle, and it had affected his eyesight. In a letter, Harriet Taylor, the woman whom Mill was to marry after the death of her first husband, says that Clark told Mill 'that a complete change and cessation from all work is absolutely necessary to save his sight.'

Mill consulted Clark again when he started coughing up blood. There was tuberculosis in his family, and his younger brother George had committed suicide the previous year in Madeira rather than wait to die slowly of consumption. Mill wrote to his wife that Clark thought he had bronchitis, 'which is the real technical name of my cough, though it sounds too large and formidable for it'—because it 'resisted all the usual remedies.'

When a little later Mill consulted Clark again he had begun to sweat at night. 'Clark thought it was chiefly from the sudden change of weather and said that almost everybody is complaining of night perspiration, the queen among others.'

A few days later, however, Clark said 'that there is organic disease of the lungs and that he had known this all along.' Had he again been trying to spare the feelings of the patient, or was he covering up his own misdiagnosis? Whatever the case, Mill evinced no indignation at the doctor's self confessed attempt at misleading his patient; in those days the doctor was evidently expected to behave like that. This is all the more striking because Mill of all men was the most devoted to the search for truth, even if he did not always find it.

It is clear that Mill never lost his faith in Clark: his philosophical scepticism did not extend to the higher reaches of the medical profession. Not only did Clark attend his mother's last illness, but when he urged Mill to go to the continent for the sake of his health during that illness, he obeyed.

In fact it was what he wanted to do in any case; and he used Clark's advice as an excuse to abandon his mother a few days before her death. He did it without acknowledging, and probably without being conscious, that that was what he was doing.

Blow your own trumpet

Modesty was once considered a virtue, but nowadays it is clearly an impediment to a successful career. We prefer—or perhaps I should say we demand—boastfulness. To judge by job applications, the world is now stuffed full of paragons whose moral commitment to the welfare of humankind is equalled only by the brilliance of their contributions to medical science.

It therefore seems to me that all medical students and young doctors should take a leaf out of Dr Williams's pamphlet, published in Shrewsbury in 1841, entitled 'An Account of Numerous Cases of Extraordinary Cures Effected by Dr Williams.'

The introduction begins:

Dr Williams begs leave to acquaint the inhabitants of Shrewsbury, its vicinity, and the public in general, that it is by particular desire of the several individuals whose names are published in this book, that their cases should be known for the benefit of the community at large... During a practice of 40 years in various parts of Great Britain, he feels it his duty to lay the following cases before the public, that the afflicted might know where to find relief.

Indeed, it would have been unethical for Dr Williams to have remained silent any longer:

I have often considered I neglected my duty, both to myself and to my fellow creatures, in withholding the following publication of the many wonderful (in some cases I might say miraculous) cures I have performed within the last 40 years in various parts of England, as well as in Shrewsbury and Shropshire.

Dr Williams often succeeded where others failed:

Often, indeed generally, when the eminent of the faculty of every available adjacent part had in vain exerted their talents and skill, yet have I, in these desperate and hopeless cases, repeatedly and frequently brought health and continued life to themselves, and joy and happiness to their despairing friends.

There follows a list of the halt and lame made whole, complete with names. Were these wholly imaginary people? No, they were almost certainly real enough. One of the cases, Richard Derrick, was wounded in the ankle and left unable to walk after many weeks in hospital. Dr Williams, however, applied a poultice that cured him, and he now lived 'at Mrs Bromley's.' In the margin someone has written—in ballpoint pen, so I suppose it must be at least 100 years later—'Benjamin Bromley's widow.' The patients are real, even if the cures are spurious.

Dr Williams was particularly good at venereal diseases:

To enumerate the thousands of cases Dr Williams has had in the cure of the Venereal Disease would fill a volume... He therefore challenges the country, within one thousand miles of Shrewsbury, to produce his equal in the cure of the Venereal Disease, in its most inveterate stages.

Here, surely, is a model for the revalidation and licensing process for the General Medical Council to consider. Every doctor should henceforth produce a pamphlet modelled on that of Dr Williams, enumerating his or her extraordinary, and indeed almost miraculous, cures or at the very least those cures effected where others have failed.

Incidentally, Dr Williams practised at a location in Shrewsbury known as the Trumpet Passage.

Slight attention

Prosecutions of doctors for manslaughter have been rising, but they are not entirely new. Indeed, the prosecution of Dr Hadwen of Gloucester, in 1924, was a cause célèbre not only in Britain but throughout the world.

Dr Hadwen was a prominent vegetarian, antivivisectionist and antivaccinationist and the founder, with William Tebb (author of *Leprosy and Vaccination*), of the London Association for the Prevention of Premature Burial. He was the model for Doctor Therne, Rider Haggard's pro-vaccination exemplar, and he was much admired by George Bernard Shaw, who called him 'the terrible Hadwen' on account of the supposed iron irrefutability of his arguments.

Dr Hadwen wrote a long antivivisection tract, *The Difficulties of Dr Deguerre*, a travel book, and many pamphlets. When asked about the part played by vivisection in the discovery of insulin, he predicted that the death rate from diabetes would rise. Like Bernard Shaw, he was an opponent of the germ theory of disease, pouring scorn on it as a superstition.

In 1924 he stood trial for the manslaughter of a girl, Nellie Burnham, in Gloucester, where he practised. He was alleged to have missed diagnosing her diphtheria, and he failed to treat her with the antitoxin that supposedly would have saved her life (he would have refused to treat her with it even if he had diagnosed diphtheria). This was an important case because the judges at the time held that a doctor was entitled to treat a patient entirely according to his own opinion, and it was up to the patients to choose a doctor with a sound opinion.

The case for the defence was that little Nellie had not died from diphtheria but pneumonia. A decisive point, apparently, was that she had risen from her bed during her illness, to obtain a drink of cold water, and walked barefoot in her nightdress on a tiled floor. This, and not diphtheria, was the cause of her pneumonia.

It seems that Dr Hadwen, who was 70 at the time, was the victim of the malice of some other doctors of the city. There is little doubt that he was correctly acquitted, for not only was the cause of death in doubt but it was far from certain that antitoxin would have saved her if she had had diphtheria.

Dr Hadwen's acquittal was immensely popular. Huge crowds gathered to cheer him; the military were on standby in case of trouble in the event of a conviction (ex-servicemen were thought particularly likely to riot). The British Union for the Abolition of Vivisection printed 10,000 copies of a transcript of the trial.

Undoubtedly, Dr Hadwen was a member of the awkward squad. A biography of him by two disciples (who call him 'our leader') published a year after his death, and entitled *Hadwen of Gloucester: Man, Medico, Martyr*, quotes a letter from him:

My success in life has depended entirely upon following my own counsels, and never paying the slightest attention to what anybody said if their views went contrary to my own.

This is indeed strange. I attribute my failure in life to precisely the same characteristic.

The boredom of everyday life

Is it possible for a writer to describe, as from the inside, an experience that he has never himself had? Can he, for example, describe what it is like to be delirious without ever having been delirious (and remembering it)? And if he does describe it, is his description worth anything; does it convey any real knowledge or insight to the reader?

Anton Chekhov (1860-1904), a doctor when delirium must have been much more common than it is today, describes both its exterior and interior, objectively and subjectively. In the story 'The Teacher of Literature,' for example, Ippolit Ippolititch, a teacher of history and geography at a local school, dies of erysipelas (bacterial skin infection) of the face after a period of delirium.

Ippolit Ippolititch is a completely unimaginative man who never in his life says anything other than what everyone already knows. When he eats, for example, he solemnly declares that, 'Man cannot live without food.' When a colleague marries, he says to him, 'Hitherto you have been unmarried and have lived alone, and now you are married and no longer single.'

Even when delirious, he is incapable of other than the dullest banalities. Just before he dies, he mutters, 'The Volga flows into the Caspian sea... Horses eat oats and hay.'

There really are people as dull as Ippolit Ippolititch. Sometimes you hear them on trains; the volume of people's voices not, alas, always being proportional to the interest of what they have to say. I know of a man whose reaction on first seeing Versailles was to wonder how they kept it clean; his wife used to turn up the radio to drown out what he was saying. As Chekhov would have known, it was tragic for them both.

But is Chekhov right that dull people have dull delirium? There is a famous passage by De Quincey in which he says that 'if a man "whose talk is of oxen" should become an opium-eater... he will dream about oxen.' Probably the question cannot be answered scientifically because there is no validated scale of dullness, which is, after all, in the eye and ear of the beholder.

In Chehkov's story 'Typhus' (a disease that also features in work by Turgenev and Sartre), a young army lieutenant called Klimov begins to feel unwell in a train compartment on his way home. He shares the compartment with a Finn whom he dislikes; he falls half asleep while beginning to become delirious:

> *The thought of Finns and Greeks produced a feeling akin to sickness all over his body. For the sake of comparison he tried to think of the French, of the Italians, but his efforts to think of these people evoked in his mind, for some reason, nothing but images of organ-grinders, naked women, and the foreign oleographs which hung over a chest of drawers at home...*

More and more confused, his thoughts become horrifying, exaggerated distortions of his recent experiences. He manages to reach home, where, when he wakes from the delirium, caused by typhus, he discovers that his beloved sister has died of the disease, which he passed on to her.

> *This terrible, unexpected news was fully grasped by Klimov's consciousness; but terrible and startling as it was, it could not overcome the animal joy that filled the convalescent. He cried and laughed, and soon began scolding because they would not let him eat.*

Only later did his joy give way to 'the boredom of everyday life.' It is difficult to believe that this story is not written from the life.

Squirmings

Everyone knows that surgeons have a special type of personality, different from, say, that of haematologists: but how do they get it?

Here is one explanation:

In early childhood an individual at three may exercise himself with tearing the limbs from insects, pulling worms apart… At fifteen he may be assistant to a butcher and learn to cut up meat. At twenty he may enter college and become an excellent student of physiology, being especially adept at vivisectional experiments. Later he goes into medicine and becomes an expert surgeon.

This description of the surgeon's progress comes from John B Watson's book, *The Ways of Behaviorism*, published in 1928. Watson (1878-1958) became famous for the so called Little Albert experiment—a nine month old boy was shown a rat and scared with a loud noise. Later the child responded with fear to the rat alone, thus exhibiting so called classical, or Pavlovian, conditioning. Watson was the founder of a school of psychology that was, in its way, as sectarian and dogmatic as psychoanalysis, taking a small element of truth and magnifying it, often with unintentional humour, into the explanation of all things human.

There was something sinister about Watson and his acolytes. Watson himself believed that baby farms might be desirable, and regarded babies and children as infinitely plastic. He thought he could turn them into anything he wanted. For him human beings were but the sum total of their conditioning, and he ends *The Ways of Behaviorism* by answering the question of whether an adult can change his personality. The answer is maybe, though it would be onerous:

Possibly if we had absolute control over food, sex, shelter, if we had some great reconditioning laboratory where the individual could be brought for a year for rigorous study and experimentation, we might be able to undo for him in a year what home nurture had done for him in thirty years.

Among the evils of 'home nurture' is mother love, every reference to which in this book is negative, being equated with smothering, stifling, and infantilising. Much better for babies to be in nice hygienic laboratories, where psychologists can blow air at their corneas and make sure that they develop no irrational fear of snakes.

Consciousness held no mystery for Watson, in part because he denied that it existed. All that mattered was behaviour, not what went on in minds (whose existence he also denied), though he does not explain why anything at all should matter if there is no consciousness and there are no minds. For him, human beings are mechanical contrivances: 'There is no mystery in building the human being into as complicated an organism as he is,' he wrote, and he looked forward to the day when 'the worst adult social failure' could be 'pulled apart and given a new set of works.'

In the meantime, regrettably, we shall go on in the same old way:

Our accomplishments, even our words and sentences, are so limited and stereotyped that you can pretty well predict what the majority of men and women are going to say and do in most situations. We are so stupidly uninteresting. We stop the [rational, behaviourist] organization of these squirmings [ie what we say and do] just as soon as we can get along with the group we live with…

By comparison with this, three year old future surgeons tearing the limbs off insects and pulling worms apart are humanity itself.

9. Shakespeare

The medical in Shakespeare's Twelfth Night

The late Susan Sontag wrote a book that decried the use of illness as metaphor, and argued that we should abandon the practice. If Shakespeare had followed her advice the plays would have been somewhat shorter, for medical metaphors are very frequently employed in them.

In *Twelfth Night*, the very name of one of the principal characters, Sir Andrew Aguecheek, is a medical reference. What would you expect of a man who suffered chronically from the ague? That he would be lean, sallow, and weak, without much in the way of willpower: precisely the character of Sir Andrew.

There is a medical metaphor in only the nineteenth line of the play. The Duke of Illyria, Orsino, describes the effect upon him of the Countess Olivia, with whom he is in love but who has retired into mourning for a brother who has just died of a cause that we never learn: 'Methought she purged the air of pestilence.' Olivia falls in love instead with Viola, disguised as a boy, who is sent to her by the Duke to woo on his behalf: 'How now? / Even so quickly may one catch the plague?'

The plague, of course, is love, but (non-metaphorically) also a disease that scholars say exercised a profound and even determining effect upon Shakespeare's literary career. But never was the effect of new found love on the lover's mind more succinctly expressed than by the Duke: 'For, such as I am, all true lovers are: / Unstaid and skittish in all matters else. / Save in the constant image of the creature / That is belov'd.'

When Feste, the Clown, or Fool, sings his famous song, 'What is love? 'Tis not hereafter; / Present mirth hath present laughter,' Sir Toby Belch (a name appropriate to his drinking habits) and Sir Andrew compliment him, for his song is catching:

Sir Andrew: A mellifluous voice, as I am true knight.
Sir Toby: A contagious breath.
Sir Andrew: Very sweet, and contagious, i'faith.

Not all the medical references in *Twelfth Night* are metaphorical, however. The caring professions are portrayed as drunken. When asked whether a forged letter suggesting that Olivia is in love with her steward, Malvolio, is having an effect upon him, Sir Toby replies: 'Like aqua-vitae [distilled spirits] with a midwife.' And when an injured Sir Toby asks the Clown whether he has called the surgeon to attend to his wounds, the Clown replies: 'O he's drunk, Sir Toby, an hour agone; his eyes / were set at eight i' the morning.' Sir Toby replies, somewhat hypocritically, 'I / hate a drunken rogue.'

There is much about madness in the play. When Olivia is told that Malvolio, unusually cheerful, has gone mad, she says: 'I am as mad as he / If sad and merry madness equal be.' Shakespeare thus recognises the twin poles of affective disorder.

When Malvolio begins to act yet more strangely Sir Toby says, 'Come, we'll have him in a dark room and bound.' And that is precisely what is done to him. Thus confined, Malvolio is visited by the Clown, in the guise of a clergyman, Sir Topaz (the precious stone was considered a cure for madness). When the Clown reveals himself as such, the following exchange takes place:

Malvolio: Fool, there was never a man so notoriously abused. I am as well in my wits, Fool, as thou art.
Clown: But as well? Then you are mad indeed, if you be no better in your wits than a fool.

In this scene Malvolio, until then a comic figure, turns into a tragic one: a moral lesson, for there is something of Malvolio's conceit in most of us.

Nameless woe: medical themes in Richard II

More has been written about Shakespeare and the law than about Shakespeare and medicine, yet you could still fill a small library with the second group; and it is my contention that every play of his contains much to interest doctors. To test this hypothesis I took one play, *Richard II*, to scan it for medical interest.

I chose *Richard II* because I found an edition for £1 in a nearby charity shop, which I thought I could mark up without a sense of guilt at the defacement. Annotations to books are always ugly and disfiguring until they are 100 years old, when they become of historical interest. It is a curious transformation.

The medical interest of *Richard II* falls into three categories: the image of doctors, the use of illness as metaphor, and clinical observation. In the play Richard II is depicted as spendthrift and feckless, in thrall to 'the caterpillars of the commonwealth,' his greedy and thoughtless courtiers. He is overthrown by his first cousin Henry Bolingbroke, who becomes Henry IV.

The play begins with the dispute between Thomas Mowbray, Duke of Norfolk, and Henry Bolingbroke, Duke of Hereford. They accuse each other of being traitors and propose to fight to settle the matter (an odd way, to our way of thinking, of deciding a matter of truth). Richard, trying to arbitrate, says:

> *'Let's purge this choler without letting blood—*
> *This we prescribe, though no physician;*
> *Deep malice makes too deep incision.*
> *Forget, forgive, conclude and be agreed:*
> *Our doctors say this is no month to bleed.'*

This is odd, because the opening of the play takes place in April, and spring was generally deemed a favourable month for therapeutic blood letting.

Although Richard speaks of physicians in this passage with respect, he not long afterwards suggests that they speed their patients on their way to death. Richard hears that John of Gaunt, 'time-honoured Lancaster,' is on his deathbed; and, ever short of money, Richard intends after his death to help himself to all his possessions. He exclaims:

'Now put it, God, in the physician's mind
To help him to his grave immediately!
Come, gentlemen, let's all go visit him,
Pray God we may make haste and come too late!'

The most pertinent clinical description in the play is that of anxiety and depression, which Richard's queen feels when she is parted from him and has an intimation of disaster. She suffers from an anxiety state:

'Some unborn sorrow ripe in Fortune's womb
Is coming towards me, and my inward soul
With nothing trembles'

One of the 'caterpillars of the commonwealth,' Sir John Bushy, who is executed before the play is over, tries to console her by telling her that 'with false sorrow's eye' she 'weeps things imaginary,' but it does not help her:

'For nothing hath begot my something grief,
Or something hath the nothing that I grieve –
But what it is that is not yet known what,
I cannot name: 'tis nameless woe, I wot [I know].'

This, surely, is an excellent description of her state of mind; and, as usual, Shakespeare is able to convey subjective experience in such a way that we almost experience it for ourselves. How did he do it? Did Shakespeare himself have anxiety? Yes, if he had been ambitious, cautious, reckless, prudent, drunken, sober, brave, cowardly, licentious, puritanical, hypocritical, honourable, foolish, wise, romantic, cynical, and a thousand other things as well.

Shakespeare on alcohol

Shakespeare knew all about drinking; he liked a drink himself. Indeed, we are told that he died after a drinking session in Stratford with Ben Jonson, though whether from alcohol poisoning, an epidemic brought on by the recent flooding in Stratford, or as a matter of coincidence, we do not know.

Perhaps, then, the scenes enacted in the centre of every British town and city on Friday and Saturday nights would not altogether have surprised him because, as Iago says to Cassio in *Othello*, 'They [the English] are most potent in potting. Your Dane, your German, and your swag-bellied Hollander—drink, ho!—are nothing to your English.'

Cassio, in fact, has a low tolerance for alcohol: 'I have very poor and unhappy brains for drinking. I have drunk but one cup tonight, and that was craftily qualified [diluted] too; and behold what innovation [confusion] it makes here. I am unfortunate in the infirmity.'

Like many a drunk, however, he tries to persuade his interlocutors that he is not really drunk (and surely Shakespeare must have heard this said, if not said it himself): 'Do not think, gentlemen, that I am drunk; this is my ancient, this is my right hand, and this is my left hand. I am not drunk now, I can stand well enough, and I speak well enough.'

But in his heart, which changes rapidly, Cassio knows well enough that he is drunk, and laments, 'O God, that men should put an enemy in their mouths to steal away their brains! That we should, with joy, pleasance, revel and applause, transform ourselves into beasts!'

Shakespeare being Shakespeare, though, knew that there were more than two answers to every question. He knew that drink had its virtues because he makes Falstaff say, of the po-faced Prince John of Lancaster, 'Good faith, this same young sober-blooded boy doth not love me, nor a man cannot make him laugh; but that's no marvel, he drinks no wine.'

This is at the beginning of Falstaff's great speech extolling sherris sack (sherry) in *Henry IV Part II*:

'A good sherris-sack hath a two-fold operation in it: it ascends me into the brain, dries me there all the foolish and dull and crudy vapours which environ it, makes it apprehensive, quick, forgetive [imaginative, able to forge ideas], full of nimble, fiery and delectable shapes, which deliver'd o'er to the voice, the tongue, which is the birth, becomes excellent wit. Who has never been cornered by a drunk who thinks that he is being witty?'

Sherris sack gives Dutch courage to the consummate coward who is Falstaff:

'It illumineth the face, which as a beacon gives warning to all the rest of this little kingdom, man, to arm; and then the vital commoners and inland petty spirits muster me all to their captain, the heart, who, great and puffed up with this retinue, doth any deed of courage; and this valour comes of sherris.'

Shakespeare even describes a rare condition, alcoholic hallucinosis; in *The Tempest*, while drinking, Stephano hears a voice (actually that of the invisible Ariel) accusing him of lying. Trinculo says to him, 'Out o' your wits, and hearing too? A pox on your bottle! This can sack and drinking do.'

Incidentally, in *The Tempest* Caliban is often taken to symbolise man in a state of nature. But really he is a psychopath, not a savage, noble or otherwise; as Prospero says of him, 'A devil, a born devil, on whose nature / Nurture can never stick; on whom my pains / Humanely taken, all, all lost, quite lost.'

Much ado about nothing

In its quiet way the Wye is one of the most beautiful rivers in the world, and the last thing anyone would wish to do is to dredge it. But this is precisely what, in 1909, Orville Ward Owen of Detroit, Michigan, did. Moreover he persuaded the Duke of Beaufort not only that it would be a good idea but to foot most of the bill for doing so.

Dr Owen, a successful physician with a large practice, became obsessed by the Baconian theory of Shakespearean authorship. He invented an elaborate cipher machine, still in existence, to collate the works of Bacon and Shakespeare and thus to discover hidden messages in them. In fact he found hidden messages everywhere, and it was in Sir Philip Sydney's *Arcadia* that he uncovered the words 'HID UNDER WYE.'

He concluded that it was the manuscripts of Shakespeare's play, in Bacon's hand, that were hidden at Chepstow. And indeed he found an ancient wooden structure as he dredged, which he thought would contain what he was looking for. Others said that it was merely a wooden pier at a place that was used as a ford across the river and pointed to an old wooden structure still standing on the opposite bank. Dr Owen was insistent, however, and concluded only that the absence of manuscripts proved that someone had got there before him. As the *New York Times* correspondent put it, 'Since his researches have become public Dr Owen has been much bothered with ridicule.'

The same correspondent was highly sceptical about the validity of the cipher: 'As I saw the cipher—a mass of letters from which it would be possible, one would imagine, to form any sentence—it spoke volumes for the patience, enthusiasm, optimism, and earnestness which Dr Owen has devoted to his life's work.'

Among other products of his life's work were new plays, allegedly by Bacon-Shakespeare, that he derived by his method. They included *The Historical Tragedy of Mary Queen of Scots* and *The Tragical History of Our Late Brother Robert, Earl of Essex*. They are composed in terrible pseudo-Elizabethan doggerel of precisely the kind that an educated man without poetic talent might compose. They are quite unreadable, unredeemed by their many absurd lines.

Poor Dr Owen. He kept the faith for a long time and went on digging until 1920. On his deathbed he realised that he would have been better to have stuck with medicine as a career:

When I discovered the Word Cipher, I had the largest practice of any physician in Detroit. I could have been the greatest surgeon there. But I thought that the world would be eager to hear what I have found. Instead, what did they give me? I have had my name dragged in the mud, lost my fortune, ruined my health, and today am a bedridden almost penniless invalid.

Of how many writers could it be said that they thought, when they started out, that the world would be eager to hear their message—only to find that it was not. By contrast, patients listen to what we doctors say with minute attention and carry out what used to be our instructions, and are now our suggestions, to the very letter.

An aural question

Doctor Johnson once said that a man is seldom so innocently employed as when he is making money. He might have added: as when he is reading or writing Shakespeare criticism. What more harmless diversion could there be for the human intellect? Not, of course, that such criticism is always free of rancour, for what would scholarship be without the edge of enmity to spur it to ever higher flights of ingenious redundancy?

J Dover Wilson's *What Happens in Hamlet*, published in 1935, is one of the most famous works of Shakespeare criticism. It starts off with a puzzle whose existence had eluded critics for three centuries, namely that of the failure of the dumb show in Act III to alarm Claudius, only for him to have a fit of guilty rage when the very same scene is enacted before him with words a few moments later.

The ghost of King Hamlet had informed Hamlet of how Claudius murdered him, and it was this murder that the dumb show re-enacted:

'Upon my secure hour thy uncle [Claudius] stole
With juice of cursed hebona in a vial,
And in the porches of my ear did pour
The leprous distilment, whose effect
Holds such an enmity with blood of man…
that it invariably kills him.'

What is hebona? The pharmacological puzzle eludes Dover Wilson, because he is not a doctor; nor does he ask whether it is possible to poison anyone to death by the aural route. (*Hamlet* has other toxicological questions: for example, the nature of the poison Laertes uses to tip his rapier with which he kills Hamlet and of the poison in the wine that kills Gertrude: laurel water, perhaps?)

I asked an eminent toxicologist friend of mine whether any poison could be absorbed from the external auditory meatus in sufficient quantity to kill instantaneously, and perhaps reassuringly he did not know.

Now it so happens that I once gave a lecture in Germany to the excellent Deutsch-Englische Gesellschaft (the society founded after the second world war to restore Anglo-German relations) on Shakespeare and medicine, in which I raised the very question of the aural route of poison. Germans love Shakespeare and also lectures about Shakespeare: my audiences (for I gave the lecture five times) were far larger than any that would have come to hear me in Britain, where I am at least equally unknown.

It was inevitable, then, that a member of the audience on one occasion should have something learned to say on the question, namely that there is a similar such case of poisoning in Castiglione's *Book of the Courtier*.

I felt like Holly Martins, the writer of pulp western novels in Graham Greene's *The Third Man*, who gives a lecture to a Viennese literary society that mistakes him for a highbrow novelist. Martins is asked by a cultivated member of the audience whether he was influenced in his work by James Joyce, of whom he has scarcely heard and has certainly never read.

I resolved to read Castiglione but regret that I have not yet done so. And what if the member of the audience had misremembered the identity of his Italian renaissance author? Does that mean that I shall have to read Benvenuto Cellini's autobiography (surely a more likely source of a story of a poisoning) and all the rest?

Can anyone save me this trouble? And is it indeed possible—in fact, not in literature—to poison someone to death by pouring a leprous distilment in their ear?

Baconians versus Stratfordians

Can anyone resist an interminable controversy that is not capable of being settled, has no practical consequences, and is argued with all the resources of erudition? Such a controversy has been caused by the theory that Francis Bacon was the real author of Shakespeare's plays, a theory first put forward over a century and a half ago by a learned American lady of the name, oddly enough, of Bacon (who soon afterwards ended her days in an asylum). It has kept many ingenious people busy ever since.

Among them was an eminent surgeon at the Royal United Hospital, Bath, called W S Melsome (1865-1944). His book, *The Bacon-Shakespeare Anatomy*, was published in 1945, the year after his death; and it is strangely comforting to know that amid the cataclysm that was the Second World War there were still people engaged on works of learning of no significance to the war effort.

Melsome was a man of two, if not three, cultures: scientific, clinical, and literary. In October 1898, during the heroic era of bacteriology, Melsome published a paper in the *BMJ* entitled, 'The value of bacteriological examination before, during, and after surgical operations'. In it he says:

I am not urging that it is necessary for the surgeon to discriminate between different kinds of micro-organisms, but I wish to point out the advantage he derives from being able to decide whether or not micro-organisms are present in the structures with which he is about to deal.

He goes on to describe a case of a woman with gonorrhoea and monoarthritis who escaped operation because the fluid in her joint was sterile.

Melsome was a man of formidable memory, learning, and intellect, and it is said that he could collate the whole of Shakespeare and Bacon from memory, without resort to texts. His method is that of finding parallels between the two sets of work so striking that they suggest the same man as the author of both: and since Bacon survived Shakespeare, and was in any case much the more learned of the two, he it was who was the author of both.

It is true that many of the parallels are striking, not only verbally but in thought. I will give only one as an example. Bacon says in his *Exempla Antithetorum*, 'If it were visible old age deforms the mind more than the body.' Here are lines from *The Comedy of Errors*: 'He is deformed, crooked, old and sere, Ill-fac'd, worse bodied, shapeless everywhere; / Vicious, ungentle, foolish, blunt, unkind, / Stigmatical in making, worse in mind.'

What this proves is, of course, a matter of opinion. The Stratfordians, as they are called by the Baconians, have not been silent. W H Saint-George, a writer on musical instruments, put forward a medical argument that Shakespeare was Shakespeare in his *Young Man From Stratford*.

One of the arguments of the Baconians—indeed of the Oxfordians, Rutlandians, and Marlovians—is that Shakespeare retired to his home town in 1611, where he seems to have indulged in no intellectual activity whatever. But, says Saint-George, consider how he had lived in London: he had worked and played too and probably contracted syphilis. He went back to Stratford after having a stroke, which also accounts for the shakiness of his signatures on his will. QED.

Of course, there are some who think that Shakespeare wrote Bacon, but that is another question.

A porcupine

The most sincere encomium to the medical profession known to me is the invariable habit of US publishers of prominently appending MD to the name of any American doctor who writes a book. The fact that the author is a doctor attests automatically to the seriousness and, above all, the veracity of the contents. Mere PhDs are not treated in the same way: for academics lie or make mistakes, but doctors never. You can always trust a doctor.

British publishers are less respectful of our great profession, but in 1947 the Vision Press published an edition of *Hamlet* with 'a psychological study by Ernest Jones MD,' whose name with degree is very nearly as prominent as that of Shakespeare and whose essay, perhaps, was the main attraction of the edition, since so many other editions were available, even in those straitened times. Dr Jones had published a paper on *Hamlet* in 1923 and went on to a book length study of Hamlet in 1949, called *Hamlet and Oedipus*.

Ernest Jones was the first British disciple of Freud, and he wrote a three volume biography, or hagiography, of him. He is accused by later scholars of having been a toady and a liar, prepared to gloss over the truth to preserve his master's heroic image and therefore (perhaps) his own. As an epigraph to his book *Papers on Psychoanalysis*, published in 1913, he quotes Freud: 'A misunderstanding is often a desire to misunderstand,' which is not so much a double edged sword as a porcupine whose prickles hurt whichever way you pick it up.

As one might expect, Jones made hay with the oedipal theme. He claims that the central problem of *Hamlet* is the reason for the protagonist's reluctance to revenge himself upon his uncle, Claudius, who murders Hamlet's father with poison and then marries Hamlet's mother, in the process becoming king.

Jones's explanation is that the actions of Claudius are, in fact, but an enactment of what Hamlet would have liked to do himself—kill his father and sleep with his mother—but which his ego and his superego forbade. Thus, in killing Claudius he would be killing himself; and indeed by the end of the play all the major characters are dead, for death was the only way to resolve Hamlet's inner conflict.

In support of his thesis Jones points out that although Hamlet's detestation of his uncle Claudius for having poisoned his father is expressed in a comparatively perfunctory way, he refers to Claudius's swift wooing of and marriage to Gertrude, his mother, in a much more emotional way. Therefore, the marriage is much more important to him than the murder.

This overlooks the fact that Claudius is, in law, a usurper of the crown, which ought, on the death of Hamlet's father (also called Hamlet), have devolved to Hamlet and not to Hamlet père's brother. This is a much more straightforward reason for Hamlet to hate Claudius than any subconscious conflict; and surely most assassins suffer from hesitations.

But how pleasant it is to dispute about unimportant and undecidable matters such as the motives of a fictional character. As a friend of mine put it when talking to someone who thought that Jones's interpretation was correct, 'I don't care if Hamlet had an Oedipus complex—so long as he loved his mother.'

A fundamental question

All's Well That Ends Well is one of Shakespeare's so called problem plays. Although normally considered a comedy, it is very nearly a tragedy, so nearly that its real genre is in doubt. Even the supposedly happy ending, which restores it to the realm of comedy, is equivocal and suspiciously perfunctory.

The play also has a medical problem. Indeed the whole plot turns on it; commentaries and introductions to various editions do not dwell on this problem much, but it is likely to preoccupy any doctor who sees or reads the play. It is the question of what kind of fistula, exactly, the king of France suffers from and how it was cured.

Helena is the daughter of a famous physician, now dead, who is part of the household of the countess of Rousillon. She is in love with the countess's son, Bertram, a somewhat callow youth who is also a fearful snob.

When he goes to Paris, she soon follows, vowing to cure the king's mortal illness, caused by a fistula, and thus raise her status enough to win Bertram. Indeed the king, initially reluctant to be treated by her, offers her the hand of any man she chooses if she cures him (the king feels he has the right to offer this). She cures him and chooses Bertram, who goes through with the marriage, but rather than consummate it he flies to the wars in Italy, vowing never to be a real husband to her. Eventually, by the usual subterfuges involving mistaken identity, Helena wins him back. The play ends with a less than ringing declaration of faith in the future of the couple by the king:

All yet seems well, and if it end so meet,
The bitter past, more welcome is the sweet.

Why is the king dying from his fistula? There is a subtle dig at the royal physicians, who have 'worn me out/With several applications' (that is, their different treatments). Anyone who has read of the way, say, that Philip II of Spain, Charles II of England, or Louis XIV were treated by their physicians will realise that a cure being worse than the disease was no mere figure of speech in those days, as no

154

doubt sometimes it is not even in our own; and perhaps Helena saved the king's life not because he was dying from fistula but because he was dying from medical treatment, from whose wilder prescriptions she desisted, replacing them with the ineffectual but harmless cure alls, 'of rare and proved effects,' bequeathed to her on his deathbed by her father.

Where is the king's fistula? To proctologists their area of the body is the seat of all happiness, and therefore of all misery, and in *Diseases of the Colon and Rectum* (1998;41:914-24) the American surgeon Bard C Cosman makes a powerful case for the fistula of the king of France having been anal. Most commentators had hitherto placed it northward in his body, usually in the breast.

There is one argument against what Dr Cosman says. Helena's treatment has restored sensation in the king's hand, which his illness had destroyed. It is difficult to see how an anal fistula could have resulted in this—unless, of course, treated with heavy metal medications and unguents (and the father of heavy metal treatments, Paracelsus, is named, though in passing, in the play).

But who can resist this conclusion of Dr Cosman, that his reading of the play 'has implications… for our view of the place of anal fistulas in cultural history'?

The wisdom of Falstaff

The government, I have read in various newspapers, wants to try bribing us into shape. Those of us who are fat will be given cash incentives to lose weight, apparently. Of course, I can quite see the logic of this: it will save the country money in the end. But perhaps an even better idea would be televised humiliation sessions for those who failed to lose weight, in front of a paying, and possibly even a baying, audience, complete with punishment for the worst offenders, as voted by the viewers. Not only would this save money in the long term, it would positively raise money in the short term. The television rights could be substantial.

Like every doctor I am against obesity, smoking, and animal fats and in favour of lentils and exercise. But once, when investigating the way people actually lived, I attended a bingo hall, which I had never done before, and saw a large number of overweight elderly people having a lovely time, smoking, drinking beer, and eating chips. It was the very antithesis of doctors' orders, and it lifted my heart to see so many people disobey us utterly.

I bet they all lied to us as well, telling us how, despite their very best efforts, the weight just wouldn't come off.

I couldn't help thinking of Falstaff. The old man—that 'whoreson obscene greasy tallow-catch'—is wholly reprehensible of course, and yet one wouldn't have him other than as he is. Excellent as uprightness and good sense are, a world in which everyone without exception was upright and sensible would be more or less intolerable.

In the bingo hall I remembered how Falstaff, playing Prince Hal to Prince Hal's King Henry in an imaginary rehearsal of Prince Hal's interview with his disapproving father, utters this encomium to himself:

That he is old, the more the pity, his white hairs do witness it, but that he is, saving your reverence, a whoremaster, that I utterly deny. If sack and sugar be a fault, God help the wicked! If to be old and merry be a sin, then many an old host I know is damned. If to be fat be to be hated, then Pharaoh's lean kine are to be loved. No, my good lord! Banish Peto, banish Bardolph, banish Poins - but for sweet Jack Falstaff, kind Jack Falstaff, true Jack Falstaff, valiant Jack Falstaff—and therefore more valiant, being as he is old Jack Falstaff—banish not him thy Harry's company, banish not him thy Harry's company. Banish plump Jack, and banish all the world.

And the strange thing is that, when he says it, we know that it is true: that a world deprived of foolishness, of gaiety for its own sake, of non-conformity to the dictates of good sense, such as is dreamed of by puritans of all stripes, whether religious or medical, would be dreary indeed.

Not that Falstaff is beyond redemption. When he claims, preposterously, to have killed Harry Hotspur himself in the battle at Shrewsbury, and hopes for an earldom or a duchy as a reward, he says: 'If I do grow great, I'll grow less, for I'll purge, and leave sack, and live cleanly as a nobleman should do.'

I think he would have been a good candidate for the government's bribery treatment.

The plague's the thing

Of all the epidemic diseases, plague is by far the most literary—or
perhaps I should say has inspired the most literature, from Boccaccio
to Camus. The inspiration of literature was not the only beneficial
effect of the disease, however: the Plague Orders of Elizabethan
England forbade Sunday indulgence in tippling, gaming, and tobacco
taking but, most important of all, prohibited 'the outrageous play at
the football.' Who, observing any modern English football crowd,
could deny that this would be a most excellent thing?

Some scholars maintain that the plague reduced Shakespeare's
output and shortened his career. Elizabethan playwrights were like
journalists: they wrote only when there was an immediate demand
for their work. The playhouses were closed frequently during the
Elizabethan and Jacobean period, once the bills of mortality showed
that more than 30 or 40 people had died of the plague in the past
week.

Other scholars have suggested that the quality of the drama fell
with the decreasing frequency of the plague, for there is nothing like
impending catastrophe to focus your thoughts on what is important
in life. ('Depend upon it, Sir,' said Doctor Johnson, 'it concentrates
a man's mind wonderfully when he knows he is to be hanged in a
fortnight.') Certainly, Shakespeare's greatest plays were written at a
time when plague was at its most frequent, if not quite its most
severe.

It is hardly surprising that writers of the time alluded often to a
disease that, at regular intervals, killed a tenth to a fifth of the
capital's population. If, in *Romeo and Juliet*, Friar John had not been
confined in a house that was suspected of harbouring the plague, the
all important letter would have reached Friar Laurence, and Romeo
would have got his girl. And the most romantic love story would
have ended with Juliet pregnant and Romeo deserting her, claiming
to need his space because the relationship just wasn't going
anywhere.

It is difficult not to believe that Shakespeare's description of the state of Scotland under Macbeth's rule does not make use of the author's experience of London during an epidemic:

> *Where sighs, and groans, and shrieks that rent the air*
> *Are made, not mark'd: where violent sorrow seems*
> *A modern extasy: the dead man's knell*
> *Is there scarce ask'd for who, and good men's lives*
> *Expire before the flowers in their caps,*
> *Dying, or ere they sicken.*

Oddly enough, the constant death knells got on people's nerves. In Ben Jonson's play *The Silent Woman*, the character Morose, a forerunner of Proust, was so exercised by the 'perpetuitie of ringing' that he was led to 'devise a roome, with double walls, and treble seelings; the windores close shut, and calk'd; and there he lives by candlelight.'

Of course, our ancestors considered that the plague was God's punishment for their sins, provoked by the popular entertainment of the day, the drama. 'The cause of plagues is sinne,' thundered one clergyman, 'if you looke to it well: and the cause of sinne are playes: therefore the cause of plagues are playes.'

Luckily, he was wrong. For if television (the 'playes' of our time) caused plagues, the bubonic and pneumonic would not be epidemic, they would be pandemically endemic, or endemically pandemic.

A foolish, fond old man

What was King Lear's diagnosis? There are two problems: firstly, he was a fictional character, and secondly, he is not available for tests or examination (a problem besetting all pathographers, though it also affords them infinite scope for pleasant speculation). So, screeds have been written in the last two centuries, but we are no nearer the truth—because there is no truth to come nearer to.

Let that not detain us. If we argued only about those matters that had a potentially definitive answer we should become boringly rational. Was Lear, then, demented, and if so was the dementia of the Alzheimer's, Lewy body, or multi-infarct type? (His variable mental states suggests the second or third.) Or was he depressed, perhaps as the result of an unresolved grief reaction to the death of his wife, mother of his three daughters? This doesn't seem likely, since he hardly mentions her, perhaps because she died so long before the action of the play starts.

Do I plump for a diagnosis? Brief psychotic episode, perhaps? Manic depressive psychosis (rapid cycling type)? Or even personality disorder?

No, I prefer not to do so, if only because of the warning of Edmund (the wicked bastard son of the Earl of Gloucester) against ascribing bad behaviour to anything other than our free decision to behave badly.

His father remarks,

These late eclipses in the sun and moon portend no good to us… Nature finds itself scourged by the sequent effects. Love cools, friendship falls off, brothers divide. In cities, mutinies; in countries, discord; in palaces, treason; and the bond cracked 'twixt son and father.

In reply to which Edmund soliloquises: 'This is the excellent foppery of the world, that, when we are sick in fortune… we make guilty of our disasters the sun, the moon and the stars; as if we were villains on necessity, fool by heavenly compulsion… and all that we are evil in, by a divine thrusting on.'

So let us just say, with Lear himself, that he was a very foolish, fond old man. For my money, the critical point is made by the Duke of Kent, when Lear has divided his kingdom between Goneril and Regan, excluding Cordelia because she will not indulge in any extravagant declarations of love for him. Kent says:

The youngest daughter does not love thee least,
Nor are those empty-hearted, who low sounds
Reverb no hollowness.

If Lear had realised this, then none of the tragedy and suffering would have ensued.

And here, it seems to me (this is a hobby horse of mine), Lear—

the play, I mean—speaks to our age directly: for is it not the case that we live in an age of emotional incontinence, when they who emote the most are believed to feel the most?

10. Gloria mundi

The greatest torture

The illnesses of the great and good have always been of interest, not only to themselves, of course, but to subsequent medical people, who amuse themselves by speculating on their nature. The very impossibility of coming to definitive conclusions is part of the fun of this pastime.

Oscar Wilde's father, the surgeon William Wilde, later Sir William, published a book in 1849 about the last illness of Jonathan Swift, entitled *The Closing Years of Dean Swift's Life*, a second edition of which was published the same year and dedicated to William Stokes, of Cheyne-Stokes breathing, Stokes-Adams attacks, and Stokes' law.

It seems clear that Swift suffered severely from Ménière's disease for much of his life, though the symptomatology had not been gathered into a disease entity at the time Wilde wrote (Ménière published his account 12 years later).

Wilde wrote the book to rescue Swift from the 'accusation' that, at the end of his life, he was mad, 'in the hope of rescuing his character from some of the aspersions which have been cast upon it.' His expressive dysphasia and decline into dementia were, Wilde said, organic affections of the brain that did not start until Swift was in his 70s. Swift had no functional mental illness but had dementia. Modern commentators tend to agree with Wilde.

In 1835 Swift's mortal remains in Dublin were dug up to preserve them from the rising water table then affecting St Patrick's Cathedral, and his skull was examined by phrenologists at the behest of the British Association for the Advancement of Science, then meeting in Dublin. In their opinion the skull showed that its owner had lacked the organ of wit in the brain and was almost mentally deficient; but as this was not really a very plausible conclusion with regard to one of the greatest wits of his age, they also concluded that his madness had altered the configuration of his skull and caused it to fall in. Wilde concluded that phrenology was nonsense.

As is well known, Swift left the great bulk of his estate to establish a lunatic asylum in Dublin, St Patrick's Hospital. He ended his *Verses on the Death of Dr Swift* with the famous lines: 'He gave what little wealth he had/To build a house for fools and mad:/And showed by one satiric touch/No nation needed it so much.'

At first the lord mayor of Dublin opposed Swift's scheme, for:

I was apprehensive that our case would soon be like England; wives and husbands trying who could first get the other to Bedlam. Many who were the next heirs to estates would try their skill to render the possessors disordered, and get them confined, and soon run them into real madness.

But he relented, seeing the necessity for Swift's scheme.

It was Wilde who laid to rest the myth, widely propagated and accepted, that Swift had been the first patient of his own hospital; it was not built until after his death. Wilde quotes the poignant story of Swift's expressive dysphasia (relayed in the first biography of Swift), of how, on struggling and failing to say something, he suddenly burst out, 'I am a fool!' This from one of the greatest masters of English prose.

Montaigne said that the greatest torture is not being able to express what is in one's soul.

And in this manner he died

Elizabeth Gaskell's biography of Charlotte Brontë, published in 1857, two years after its subject's death, caused a controversy and produced the threat of several libel actions (there were changes to the second edition). One of the reasons for the controversy was Mrs Gaskell's description of Miss Brontë's death, which was thought at the time to be indecently graphic. Recently married, Charlotte Brontë was pregnant:

She was attacked by new sensations of perpetual nausea, and ever-recurring faintness... A wren would have starved on what she ate during those last six weeks... Martha [her maid] tenderly waited on her... and from time to time tried to cheer her with the thought of the baby that was coming.

From this it seems that she died of hyperemesis gravidarum (extreme morning sickness), though her death certificate said phthisis (TB), which is certainly what her sisters Emily and Anne died of. These two sisters had a distinctively different attitude to medical attention: Emily refused it completely; Anne accepted it. Of Emily, Charlotte wrote only eight days before her death, 'her repugnance to seeing a medical man continues immutable,—as she declares 'no poisoning doctor' shall come near her.'

Anne was altogether more tractable. She took all that was prescribed because 'she was too unselfish to refuse trying means, from which, if she herself had little hope of benefit, her friends might hereafter derive a mournful satisfaction.' The means in question were cod liver oil: 'She perseveres with the cod-liver oil, but still finds it very nauseous,' wrote Charlotte, the doctors having thus added to her symptomatology without saving her life: an old, but I hope not continuing, tradition.

At the beginning of the biography, Mrs Gaskell illustrates the forthright nature of the Yorkshire people among whom the Brontë sisters were born with a couple of anecdotes.

We [Mr and Mrs Gaskell] were driving along the street, when one of those ne'er-do-well lads who seem to have a kind of magnetic power for misfortunes, having jumped into the stream that runs through the place, just where all the broken glass and bottles are thrown, staggered naked and nearly covered with blood into a cottage before us. Besides receiving another bad cut in the arm, he had completely laid open the artery, and was in a fair way of bleeding to death—which, one of his relations comforted him by saying, would be likely to 'save a deal o' trouble.'

Then there was a squire who 'died at his house, not many miles from Haworth' (the Brontës' home):

His great amusement and occupation had been cock-fighting. When he was confined to his chamber with what he knew would be his last illness, he had his cocks brought up there, and watched the bloody battle from his bed. As his mortal disease increased, and it became impossible for him to turn so as to follow the combat, he had looking-glasses arranged in such a manner, around and above him, as he lay, that he could still see the cocks fighting. And in this manner he died.

This was hardly an instance of the good death of which our medieval ancestors once spoke, but of which we speak no longer. The modern equivalent of the Yorkshire squire's death, I suppose, would be to die while playing a video game and sending last messages on Facebook.

Nil by mouth

Do philosophers choose their philosophy, or do their philosophies choose them? Did Hume die an equable death, for example, because of his philosophy, or did his famous even temperedness lead him to his philosophy of ironic stoicism with which his death was consonant?

One philosopher whose thought seems to have been determined by her temperament was Simone Weil (1909–43). She was a brilliant pupil and student, and one of those intimidatingly gifted children who master ancient Greek at a very early age (another was John Stuart Mill, who famously said in his autobiography that he thought it would have been better if he had learnt less Greek and played more cricket).

Simone Weil's upbringing was at least as odd as Mill's. Her father was a successful doctor, and Eli Metchnikoff, the Nobel Prize winning microbiologist who discovered phagocytosis by white cells, was a family friend. Her mother had a morbid fear of germs, so that she would not allow anyone outside the family to kiss her children, a fear that she successfully communicated to her daughter, who subsequently disdained physical contact with anyone. Her brother became one of the greatest mathematicians of the 20th century.

Perhaps Weil's temperament is best illustrated by the fact that at the age of 6 she decided she should not eat sugar because the soldiers at the front didn't have any (a little like what many of us were told as children: that we should eat up what was on our plates because there were many starving people in the world). To the end of her life she was one of those people who believed she had no right to enjoy anything unless everyone in the whole wide world could enjoy it, and this view led to an exaggerated asceticism despite the great wealth of her parents.

Having been some kind of Marxist, she became a Christian mystic, though not an orthodox one by the standards of the Catholic Church. She was always absolutist and uncompromising, carrying her views to their rationalised but nevertheless illogical conclusions. The one constant of her life seems to have been her anorexia, though her reasons for not eating properly changed according to circumstances.

She managed to join the Free French in England during the war, but died a year later of starvation and tuberculosis, and according to the coroner 'the deceased did kill and slay herself while the balance of her mind was disturbed.' She wouldn't eat any more, she said, than the people of France ate under the occupation, and developed a convoluted theological justification for her decision. It seems to me that an excess of humility soon enough becomes its opposite, spiritual pride; and for myself, I find in Weil a spiritual pride almost megalomaniac in its proportions.

In my clinical career I saw a few patients starve themselves to death by refusal to eat. It is an agonising process to watch for all concerned, from the relatives to the nurses and doctors. There is no evidence that Simone Weil, sometimes regarded as saintly, ever gave a fraction of a moment's thought to this rather obvious con-sideration.

Either the balance of her mind was disturbed, or she was very far from saintly.

Familiarity breeds contempt

In his essay *How the Poor Die*, published in 1946, George Orwell describes his admission to a hospital in Paris, which he coyly calls Hôpital X, in 1929, when he had pneumonia. He is treated unceremoniously, with cupping and a mustard plaster; the people applying these useless treatments do not bother with such refinements as informed consent—or indeed consent of any kind. The patients are lucky to get what they are given.

Orwell relates how the doctors and medical students exchange hardly a word with the patients and certainly do not acknowledge their common humanity. The students tremble with excitement as they approach Orwell, not because he is a famous writer (at that stage he wasn't) but because he exhibits a particular physical sign beautifully and it is their one chance to elicit it.

Could things really have been as bad as this? I think they probably could. Some decades after Orwell's experience I was admitted briefly to a very famous specialised hospital. One day the professor arrived, surrounded by an enormous entourage of people at various stages of their education and training. They gathered around the bed opposite mine, and the professor prefaced his remarks to them on the terrible complications the patient was likely soon to suffer with the memorable words to him, 'Now don't you listen to any of this.' The professor did not explain quite else what the patient was supposed to do (perhaps a crossword?).

In our own way we still visit humiliations on patients who do not pay, just as in Orwell's Hôpital X. An acquaintance of mine, a man of some intellectual and financial substance, was admitted to a ward of a district hospital with pneumonia, like Orwell. The staff all addressed him not by his first name alone but by a diminutive of his first name, repeating it at every opportunity to emphasise the fact that, as far as they were concerned, he was now a minor.

His wife, appalled by the lack of privacy and quiet, insisted that he be moved to a room in the private wing. The very moment he passed through the doors connecting the two parts of the hospital he became Mr Smith instead of Billy, which suggests that those who teach nurses and doctors to address patients in familiar fashion must be perfectly well aware of the continued social meaning of forms of address. Familiarity breeds contempt and is intended to do so.

Another passage from Orwell reminded me that some things change slowly. Hôpital X was so horrible that prisoners who were brought to it for treatment soon asked to be returned to prison. Now, in my experience prisoners brought into hospital fall into two classes: those who have faked or manufactured an illness to fulfil an assignation there, and those who are genuinely ill. Most of the second type ask to be returned to prison as soon as possible, and sometimes sooner. Whether this reflects more on our hospitals or our prisons—or on both equally—I am not quite sure.

The last laugh

I have always regarded critics of the medical profession as ill informed, ill intentioned, or ill adjusted—or, of course, all three. I have known several newspaper editors, for example, who were profoundly anti-doctor, a hostility I ascribe to the fact that doctors are held in far higher public esteem than journalists. If journalists cannot improve their own reputation, they can at least try to destroy that of others. Politicians are of the same ilk as journalists.

Of the great critics of the medical profession, none was more ferocious and uncompromising than Jean-Baptiste Poquelin, better known as Molière. The last play he wrote was *Le Malade Imaginaire*, and as usual he makes fun of doctors in it. The hero, or protagonist, is Argan, the hypochondriac who is completely under the sway of his doctor, Monsieur Purgon.

The opening scene has Argan adding up his apothecary's bills for all the clysters, pills, potions, electuaries and so forth that he has been prescribed and has dutifully taken. He remarks that the bill is so exorbitant that henceforth no one will want to be ill. But his faith in medicine remains absolute. 'This month,' he says, 'I have taken eight mixtures and 12 clysters; last month I took 12 mixtures and 20 clysters. No wonder I don't feel as well this month as last.' Argan says he will tell Monsieur Purgon so that he can put matters right.

It so happens that on my way to work I used to pass an establishment, in appearance halfway between a hairdressing salon and an adult bookshop, that advertised colonic irrigations as the key to wellbeing. Some illusions, it seems, die hard.

Towards the end of the play, Argan's brother, Béralde, who is not a believer in medicine, tries to wean him from his dependence on doctors. He advises him that it would be a good thing if he were to attend some of Molière's plays on the subject of doctors and medicine. Argan exclaims:

Devil take it! If I were only a doctor, I would revenge myself on his [Molière's] impertinence. When he fell ill, I would let him die without assistance. He could say what he liked, I wouldn't prescribe even the slightest blood letting for him, the smallest enema, and I would say to him, 'Die! Die! That will teach you another time to make fun of the Faculty!'

To Béralde medicine is nothing more than a confidence trick: 'You have only to speak in a cap and gown, and gibberish becomes scholarship and the greatest nonsense wisdom.'

As often happens—it is the saving of the profession—the doctors had the last laugh. Molière acted Argan in the first four performances of *Le Malade Imaginaire*, but he collapsed on stage during the fourth and died within hours without benefit of medicine.

Of course, nothing that the Faculty could have prescribed would have saved him. One has only to read of the treatment meted out by doctors to dying monarchs such as Philip II, Louis XIV, and Charles II to realise that Molière didn't miss much; quite the contrary. But faith in medicine is not proportional to its efficacy—it might even be inversely proportional to its efficacy. I wonder what evidence-based medicine has to say on this subject?

Fatal attraction

According to Gorky, Lenin feared the music of Beethoven because it made him want to pat people's heads, and this was a distraction from having them shot, which was so much more constructive.

Tolstoy had a similar, though of course not identical, reaction to Beethoven, in so far as the character of Pozdnyshev in the story The Kreutzer Sonata may be taken to express Tolstoy's own views (as I think it may). The Kreutzer causes 'an awakening of energy and feeling unsuited both to the time and place...' and 'cannot but act harmfully.'

In the story, Pozdnyshev kills his wife because he believes she has formed a liaison with a violinist, recently returned from Paris (a sure sign of depravity), with whom she plays the sonata.

From the medical point of view, what is interesting about the story is Tolstoy's vicious hatred of doctors, whom he regarded as corrupters of the world. He accused them of materialism, and indirectly of having been responsible for the murder. It was they, after all, who told the victim how to go about having sexual relations without risk of pregnancy, thus arousing her husband's insensate jealousy.

You can almost see Tolstoy, who wrote the story in his self determined role of prophet, foaming at the mouth when he spoke of doctors:

They have ruined my life as they have ruined and are ruining the lives of thousands and hundreds of thousands of human beings... It is impossible to number all the crimes they commit. But all these crimes are as nothing compared to the moral corruption of materialism they introduce into the world, especially through women.

By this stage in his life, Tolstoy was opposed to sex, and was fighting a war against it, which so far he appears to have lost. He was not the only Russian of this mind: the sect called the Skoptsi castrated themselves in their struggle against sensuality. It is not surprising that Tolstoy objected to the fact that doctors treated syphilis as a mere disease, and not the root cause of syphilis, which was sexual desire and the resultant intercourse.

Another great Russian writer, Chekhov, a doctor, was incensed by what Tolstoy wrote. In a letter to A N Pleshtcheyev in the year after the story's publication, Chekhov recognised its literary merits: 'Among all the mass that is written now, one could scarcely find anything else as powerful both in the gravity of its conception and the beauty of its execution.' But, he continued,

> ... it has one fault for which one cannot readily forgive the author—that is, the audacity with which Tolstoy holds forth about what he doesn't know and is too obstinate to care to understand. Thus his statements about syphilis... are not merely open to dispute, but show him up as an ignoramus who has not, in the course of his long life, taken the trouble to read two or three books written by specialists.

Shall I be accused of the same fault when I quote something that Tolstoy says in connection with doctors that, my agreement with Chekhov notwithstanding, does strike me as true:

> Today one can no longer say, 'You are not living rightly, live better.' One can't say that to oneself or to anyone else. If you live a bad life, it is caused by the abnormal functioning of your nerves, etc. So you must go to the doctors, and they will prescribe eight penn'orth of medicine from a chemist, which you must take!

Metaphysics and murder

Metaphysics, said the philosopher F H Bradley, is the finding of bad reasons for what we believe upon instinct. Nowadays, however, it seems more to be the finding of bad reasons for what we disbelieve on instinct.

In my youth I used to read metaphysics with an excitement that now seems to me strange and that I cannot recapture. Nevertheless, I have returned a little to philosophy, reading it in a desultory fashion according to what books I find in charity or second hand bookshops. Recently, for example, I found Peter Singer's *The Expanding Circle: Ethics and Sociobiology*, published in 1981.

Singer is an Australian philosopher (whose mother was a doctor) who sprang to fame with his book *Animal Liberation* (1975), a powerful polemic that drew attention, among other things, to the cruelty entailed in the mass production of meat. He went on to pronounce controversial views about abortion and, in particular, infanticide, and euthanasia. The criterion of whether it is permissible to end a person's life should not be whether he was alive, but whether he exhibited the attributes of so called personhood; that is to say, rationality, autonomy, and self consciousness. This would seem to make it permissible to kill people while they sleep; however, I am no philosopher.

In *The Expanding Circle*, Singer expounds a view of ethics that would undermine or destroy most medical practice, at least in a relatively rich country such as Britain. Ethical thought, he says in this book, has—since the dawn of thought—expanded the locus of its concern, rather like the ripples in a bowl of water that, from a central disturbance, eventually affect the whole surface of the liquid. At one time we believed that only our group—whether it be our family, our tribe, our village, our town, our country, our coreligionists, our race, our class, or our species—was the proper object of our ethical concern and behaviour, and only its good should concern us in our ethical decision making.

But, says Singer repeatedly, ethical thinking (and conduct) requires that we now include all sentient beings in our concern, and that the interests of no one, including ourselves, should count for more than the interests of any other sentient being merely by virtue of proximity to us. It is our duty to maximise the fulfilment of as many interests as possible; thus if I have the choice between contributing to famine relief or buying an antiquarian book, I should do the former, for the interests of the starving count more than my interest in possession of said book.

To some people, this view might seem humane and generous of spirit, but actually it would sanction (if, impossibly, it were put into practice) the greatest cruelty, and destroy civilisation and all hope of progress into the bargain. A surgeon who saved someone's life with a technically complex and costly technique would not be a hero but a villain (and let us remember that routine medical care in a country such as Britain is costly by comparison with what is available in much of the world). The surgeon could not defend himself by saying that he relieved suffering where he found it, namely in the vicinity of his hospital; he should have been using his skill, and the resources, to relieve a much greater amount of suffering elsewhere. Far from being a saviour, he is in fact a murderer.

171

11. The Imagination

Agatha Christie's doctors

Agatha Christie's novels have a lot of doctors, an inordinate number of them murderers. In *Cards on the Table* (1936) Dr Roberts is not the only villain of the piece, but he is certainly one of the villains of the piece.

The story is convoluted, but to object that it is implausible is like objecting that the story of *Little Red Riding Hood* is implausible. Fairy stories are not to be confused with social realism, any more than revolutions are to be confused with dinner parties. Indeed, in Christie's novels dinner parties are not to be confused with dinner parties.

Mr Shaitana is a foreign socialite in London who, like many rich people with not much to do, likes flirting with evil. He holds a dinner party, inviting not only Hercule Poirot and Superintendent Battle of Scotland Yard but also four seemingly respectable people whom Mr Shaitana, but no one else, knows to have committed murder. Before the evening is over one of them has killed the host for fear that he is about to be exposed.

Among the four is Dr Roberts. When he arrives he

> *... did so with a kind of parody of a brisk bedside manner. He was a cheerful, highly-coloured individual of middle age. Small twinkling eyes, a touch of baldness, a tendency to embonpoint and a general air of well-scrubbed and disinfected medical practitioner. His manner was cheerful and confident. You felt that his diagnosis would be correct and his treatments agreeable and practical.*

I don't think anyone would write a passage like this nowadays. No doubt if it referred to a male member of the profession the touch of baldness and the tendency to embonpoint could stay but not, surely, the twinkly cheerful confidence. These days Dr Roberts would have had a hard day staring at the computer screen and entering data, and he would drag himself in rather than enter briskly.

Some years ago Dr Roberts was thought by one of his patients to be having an affair with his wife and was threatened with exposure to the authorities. Dr Roberts disposed of the patient by putting anthrax in his badger hair shaving brush and of his wife by giving her typhoid rather than vaccinating her against it when she proposed to go to Egypt.

It is he who kills Mr Shaitana; he also kills one of the other suspects with an intravenous injection of N-methyl-cyclohexenyl-methyl-malonyl urea.

In investigating Dr Roberts's background Superintendent Battle questions his receptionist, Miss Burgess, about the death rate of his patients:

'From the statistical point of view, it would be interesting to know how many deaths occur among a doctor's practice per year. For instance now, you've been with Dr Roberts some years—'

'Seven.'

'Seven. Well, how many deaths have there been in that time off-hand?'

'Really, it's difficult to say.' Miss Burgess gave herself up to calculation. 'Seven, eight—of course, I can't remember exactly—I shouldn't say more than thirty in the time.'

Ah, if only we'd paid more attention to Miss Christie we should have had revalidation a long time ago: though, of course, no one claimed that Dr Roberts was actually incompetent.

Character assassination

Doctors have been murderers in literature, as in life. Among the former is Dr Charles Alavoine in Georges Simenon's *Letter to My*

Judge, published in 1947. The book is in the form of a letter addressed by Alavoine to his *juge d'instruction*, explaining why he strangled his lover. There is a short appendix, in the form of a newspaper report describing how, because of his good behaviour in prison and his professional qualifications, Dr Alavoine was given duties in the prison hospital. This allowed him access to the poisons cupboard, and he then took a fatal dose of its contents.

Dr Alavoine was not a leading light of our profession. Once qualified, he rarely looked at a medical journal, though he sometimes sneaked out of his consulting room in the small town where he practised to read his textbooks to find out how to treat a patient. He claimed, however, to have an instinct for illness; that is to say something that is almost as important as knowledge: he intuited when a condition was serious and when it would cure itself.

He bought his first practice from Dr Marchandeau, who was nearly blind. Dr Marchandeau gave him a little paternal advice:

They [the patients] are almost all the same. Above all don't tell them that a glass of water will do them as much good as medicine. They won't have any confidence in you and, what is more, at the end of the year you'll have earned hardly enough to pay your taxes and your subscriptions. Medicines, my friend, medicines!

He continues, 'They're not asking to be cured but to be looked after... And above all never say to them that they're not ill... You'll be lost if you do.' To this day, French doctors are prone to polypharmacy.

Dr Alavoine is married to a woman whom he does not love and who does not love him. After 10 years he meets a young woman called Martine in a bar in Nantes, who has had a chequered and perhaps unsavoury past. He falls instantly and passionately in love with her, and by various subterfuges manages to introduce her into his household as an employee. Inevitably his wife discovers their real relationship, and Alavoine decides to leave with Martine for Paris.

Alavoine is intensely jealous of Martine, not because she is unfaithful but because of her past, because he is not the only man to have slept with her. Several times he punches her when he thinks of this, and, according to him, she accepts the blows with humility. He comes to the conclusion that he must kill her to cancel out her sordid past and to return her to a state of innocence, in which their love will be forever perfect. As he strangles her, she looks at him first with fear, but then with 'a look of resignation and deliverance, a look of love.'

What is alarming about this is that so much of the story is auto-biographical. Simenon, like Dr Alavoine, was married to a wife whom he did not love and took a woman with whom he had a violent, jealous relationship into his household on the pretext of employing her. Like Martine, she had both a past and a large scar across her abdomen attesting to that past. Simenon didn't kill her, of course, confining himself later to mere character assassination in his books. But it was always Simenon's point that the dividing line between the killer and those who do not kill was much finer than usually supposed. Apparently, he knew; he was Dr Alavoine.

Authentic fiction

How realistic does a work of literature have to be before it is a work of realism? Do the events it relates have to be symbolic, representative, or emblematic of some wider social reality, or is it enough that unique events, for example, those of a love or murder story, should be depicted with a degree of verisimilitude?

These questions came to mind as I read the blurb on the cover of the US edition of Joan Fleming's novel *Kill or Cure*, published in 1968: 'The inside glimpse of a doctor's life is quite authentic, since the author knows this background from personal experience.' Later we learn that Joan Fleming (1908-1980), author of 33 novels, 'lives with her husband, a London physician'—actually an ophthalmic surgeon.

If I had been her husband I am not altogether sure if I should have been pleased or reassured by the claims made for the authenticity of the book. Its protagonist, Dr Jeremy Fisher, is a general practitioner in the stockbroker belt of Surrey. His wife, Iris, is a nymphomaniac who, it turns out, has slept with both of his partners in the practice. She is also having an affair with a local businessman by the name of Elland Bridge, to whose house Dr Fisher is called at the beginning of the book.

When he gets there he finds a young woman dead in bed from a botched illegal abortion. This young woman also had an affair with Elland Bridge, claimed to be pregnant by him, and had a backstreet abortion in London at his expense. After the botched operation, she had taken a taxi to his house where she promptly died.

Mrs Fisher, carrying on her affair with Bridge, was present in the house when the young woman died, and suggests (before she drives away) that Bridge call her husband to the house and accuse him of having performed the illegal operation himself, and thereby of having killed the young woman. She hopes by this means to disembarrass herself of a husband whom she detests.

When Dr Fisher learns that his wife has put Bridge up to making this accusation, he decides to retaliate by killing her with an injection of a new drug called Talbulodin. He then dumps her body in a local pond.

This forms the medical background that the author allegedly knows from personal experience. I do not consider that I have led a completely uneventful life, but compared with the goings on in Virginia Water circa 1968, it has been a very tame, almost monastic, existence.

The portrait of the doctor in the book is not very flattering: his hobby and passion, for example, is performing pharmacological experiments on patients without their knowledge or consent. He prescribes barbiturates to those who complain just to shut them up. He drives while drunk and drinks at lunchtime.

Of course, times were different then. Dr Fisher's partners are afraid that if the patients knew of his wife's sexual antics they would desert the practice in moral disgust. Husbands in those days 'gave' wives divorces by arranging to be caught in adultery specially arranged for the purpose. Mrs Fisher has a mink coat and a crocodile bag (illegal now) and wears gloves when she goes out. But it is a time of rapid change: the back street abortion is soon to be a thing of the past, and it turns out that Dr Fisher has not really killed his wife, only hallucinated that he has done so under the influence of LSD slipped into his drink at a cocktail party. Very 1968.

An awful wife

The only objective of a writer, said the critic Cyril Connolly, is to write a masterpiece. This is nonsense, of course, unless it is made true by definition: that no writer who does not aim at one is really a writer. Nevertheless it is undeniable that most writers would prefer to have written a masterpiece than not to have written one, in which case Anthony Berkeley Cox (1893-1971) ought to have died fulfilled—though almost certainly he did not, for he wrote no fiction for the last 32 years of his life.

His masterpiece, published in 1931 under the pseudonym Francis Iles, was *Malice Aforethought*. The hero of this book, or perhaps I should say protagonist, is a doctor: Dr Edmund Alfred Bickleigh. The book begins: 'It was not until several weeks after he had decided to murder his wife that Dr Bickleigh took any steps in the matter.'

Dr Bickleigh, a general practitioner in the genteel fictional Devonshire village of Wyvern's Cross, is eventually acquitted of the one murder he did commit but hanged for one he did not. Justice of a kind, therefore, is done.

No Freudian, as far as I am aware, has as yet made much of the fact that Cox's father, like the father of so many writers, was a doctor and that the execution of Dr Bickleigh might therefore be considered the symbolic fulfilment of an Oedipal wish. Moreover, Dr Bickleigh's small size and physical insignificance might likewise be deemed the author's Oedipal revenge upon his father.

In fact, Dr Bickleigh strongly resembles Dr Crippen, though his methods look forward to those employed by Dr John Bodkin Adams.

As a man who recognises his 'wormhood,' Dr Bickleigh tries to compensate by philandering, at which he is surprisingly successful. His method of disposing of Julia, his snobbish and shrewish wife, in the vain hope of marrying the rich young woman who is his current inamorata is first to give her headaches by means of a proprietary drug called Farralite, surreptitiously sprinkling it on her food, then to addict her to the morphine that he gives her to relieve those headaches, and finally to kill her with an overdose. One cannot help wondering whether Dr Bodkin Adams had read *Malice Aforethought* before embarking on his career in Eastbourne.

Mrs Bickleigh is one of the most splendidly awful wives in literature. She considers herself socially superior to her husband:

> *Before her marriage Mrs Bickleigh had been a Crewstanton. She was, in everything but name, a Crewstanton still… During their short engagement she had informed her fiancé not once, but several times, that her grandmother would no more have contemplated sitting down to a meal with her doctor than with her butler.*

Dr Bickleigh, hen pecked by his wife, is always falling in love with a different young woman:

> *He did not doubt that she was the young woman in the world whom he ought to have married. The fact that he had been looking for this one woman so long made his discovery all the more poignant; the fact that he had been certain so often before of having found her elsewhere did not affect the matter in the least.*

Malice Aforethought is as much a brilliant comedy of manners as a crime novel and as much a depiction of self deception as a comedy of manners. It therefore repays close study: for men were deceivers ever, both of themselves and others.

Forensic obsessions

Though my favourite crime novel is *Malice Aforethought,* its plot had been used before—by an author whose brother was a doctor and who had once been a medical student himself. However, he did not complete his studies because, unlike quite a few who did complete theirs, he realised he was not cut out to be a doctor. He was C S Forester (1899-1966), whose real name was Cecil Louis Troughton Smith, and who became best known for the Horatio Hornblower series of novels.

The book in question is *Payment Deferred,* a psychological thriller set in the dismal lower middle class suburbs of south London, published in 1926. The protagonist, Mr Marble, is a minor employee in the foreign exchange department of a bank in the city. He is perpetually hard up, partly because he drinks too much, and a crisis is approaching. He sees his opportunity when a rich nephew from Australia turns up unexpectedly. Mr Marble's hobby is photography, and he poisons his nephew with his supply of prussic acid, which he slips into the whisky he gives him. He buries his nephew in the small back garden of number 47, Malcolm Road.

Thereafter Mr Marble spends all his spare time watching the garden, afraid that someone will come in and discover the body; he drinks even more; and he becomes obsessed by forensic medicine, accumulating books on the subject though previously he was not a great reader.

His wife, who loves him distractedly even though he is far from an ideal husband, discovers that his copy of *A Handbook of Medical Jurisprudence* falls open on a certain well thumbed page—that relating to poisoning by potassium cyanide. Having wondered about the strange disappearance of the nephew, she guesses the truth: her husband has murdered him.

Mrs Marble tries to keep her knowledge to herself, but Mr Marble realises that she knows. A silence falls between them. Then Mrs Marble discovers that her husband was once unfaithful to her: she commits suicide with potassium cyanide, and Mr Marble is hanged for it. The death of the nephew is never discovered.

Oddly enough there was a book titled *A Handbook of Medical Jurisprudence* current at the time that Forester wrote *Payment Deferred*. It was by William Alfred Brend (1873-1944), and went through at least 10 editions. Its description of the symptoms and signs of potassium cyanide poisoning was very similar to that found by Mrs Marble in her husband's *Handbook*.

Brend was a barrister and a lecturer in forensic medicine at the Charing Cross Hospital. His interests were wide, to judge by the titles of his books: from *An Inquiry into the Statistics of Deaths from Violence and Unnatural Causes in the United Kingdom; with Special Reference to Deaths from Starvation, Overlying of Infants, Burning, Administration of Anaesthetics, and Poisoning* (1915) to *Sacrifice to Attis: a Study of Sex and Civilization* (1936).

By a very strange coincidence, my copy of his *A Handbook of*

Medical Jurisprudence falls open on page 278, on which are described the symptoms and signs of poisoning by potassium cyanide.

Closely observed humans

All art, said Walter Pater, aspires to the condition of music. Whether this be so or not, the Swiss novelist and dramatist, Friedrich Dürrenmatt (1921-90) certainly wrote the novel *The Assignment: or, on the Observing of the Observer of the Observers* after listening to a recording of Glenn Gould playing the first half of Bach's *The Well-Tempered Clavier*. He decided then to write a novel in 24 sentences, either in imitation or in honour of Bach; not surprisingly the book is short, but the sentences are long.

It is a technical accomplishment to write a sentence several pages long that is both lucid and easy to follow, and Dürrenmatt succeeds triumphantly. The novel is a metaphysical thriller, a meditation on the increasingly convoluted ways in which we are all, in the modern world, under surveillance.

The story opens when the wife of an eminent psychiatrist, Dr Otto von Lambert, suddenly disappears, and her strangled and raped body is found some months later at some ruins in the desert in an unnamed north African country (which is obviously Morocco). Why has she fled; why has she been killed?

The answer appears to be that she has discovered the clinical notes that her husband has been making on her state of depression. He attributes this to the existential nullity of human existence, and could have written the same of anyone. His observations are entirely abstract and without emotion, as if observing someone with whom he has no relationship and for whom he cares nothing. He defines her depression as:

> … *a psychosomatic phenomenon resulting from insight into the meaningless-ness of existence, which is inherent in existence itself, since the meaning of existence is existence, which insight, once accepted and affirmed, makes existence unbearable, so that Tina's [his wife's] insight into that insight was the depression.*

What the good doctor does not realise is that his wife is simultaneously recording her own observations of him, but hers by comparison with his are extremely concrete, and thus disparaging in quite another way.

Her observations:

... had portrayed him as a monster, virtually peeling pieces off him, facet by facet, examining each one separately, as if under a microscope, constantly narrowing and magnifying the focus and the sharpening of the light, page after page about his eating habits, page after page about the way he picked his teeth.

No one's character could survive such minute observation; everyone would appear disgusting viewed this close up. 'One could not [afterwards] help imagining that [one] is disgusting to look at while eating'—or, of course, doing any of the other necessary things observed in the same way.

In other words, not to be observed at all, to be reduced to mere abstractions, is demeaning because it implies a lack of human interest on the part of the non-observer; but on the other hand, to be too closely or obsessively observed, to have nothing overlooked, is to feel oneself simultaneously trapped, repellent, and despicable.

There is a level of observation, then, that is correct, somewhere between absent and minute, but it differs according to the situation and is therefore always a matter of judgment. And where judgment is, error is sure to follow.

Behind the wit

It often seemed to me during my clinical career that some people were called upon (by what, or by whom?) to bear more suffering and loss than was their fair share, or more than could be explained by anything that they, or indeed anyone else, had done. Tragedy followed them around like an obedient dog; mostly they bore it unprotestingly. They made me feel guilty because I was in the habit of complaining so vociferously about the minor inconveniences of life.

The American writer Peter De Vries (1910-93) was in general

known for his comic novels and for his wit—he once said that he enjoyed being a writer, except for the paperwork. But one of his novels, *The Blood of the Lamb*, published in 1961, was bleak and tragic—and autobiographical.

De Vries was born of Dutch Calvinist stock to whom (as he later put it) everything was forbidden except heaven. In the novel, his narrator-protagonist's older brother, a medical student, dies of pneumonia; a girlfriend dies of tuberculosis; his father goes mad and dies in an asylum; his wife commits suicide; and his daughter dies aged 12 of acute leukaemia. Quite a lot of this happened, more or less; and though De Vries was famously antireligious, it is clear that he was still wrestling with his own religious upbringing 50 years after his birth.

His depiction of doctors is not altogether flattering. The family doctor of the narrator's childhood, Doc Berkenbosch, is an ignoramus who attended one of the worst medical schools in the United States before they were properly regulated, and didn't even master medical vocabulary, calling, for example, ulcers 'ulsters,' and the peritoneum the 'plethora.'

The psychiatrist who attends his wife shortly before she commits suicide 'could do no more than apply a poultice of polysyllables to a wound he could neither see nor understand any better than the next man'; but for sheer insensitivity it would be difficult to beat Dr Scoville, the great leukaemia expert, who talks breezily of the treatment of this then invariably fatal disease as if it were a game:

> *I'd like to start her on the 6-MP [6-mercaptopurine], but it needs a few weeks to take hold, and I don't know whether we have the time. She's pretty explosive. But let's try it. If things get tricky we'll just pop her into hospital and dose her with cortisone. We like to keep the steroids for later, an ace in the hole.*

Perhaps this was the most difficult time for parents to have a child with leukaemia, when treatment to produce remission but not a lasting cure had become available. At any rate, it explains the conversation that the narrator has with the father of another child undergoing treatment. The narrator says to him that at least medicine can now produce a remission. He replies,

> *'So death by leukemia [sic] is now a local [train] instead of an express. Same run, only a few more stops. But that's medicine, the art of prolonging disease.'*
> *'Jesus,' I said, with a laugh. 'Why would anyone want to prolong it?'*
> *'In order to postpone grief.'*

Peter De Vries's daughter died of leukaemia aged 11 years in 1960. By the time he himself died, such childhood leukaemia was often curable. Would this have comforted or embittered him? At any rate, it was thanks to the likes of Dr Scoville that it was so.

Impostors without the syndrome

However hard it is to be a doctor, it must be much harder to be a medical impostor. Not only must you do a good imitation of being a doctor, and therefore suffer all the anxieties that a genuine doctor suffers, but you must also suffer the constant fear of exposure, ridicule, and retribution that goes with any impostor's part.

Of course, many if not most doctors must have felt at times that they are impostors, when they tell patients things that are beyond their knowledge or provide reassurance not entirely based upon the truth. And I dare say we all know doctors of limited capacity who nevertheless exude an air of authority to which we do not believe that they are entitled, though it may fool some patients. On examination, then, the distinction between an authority and an impostor turns out to be a little like that between hypertension and normotension, a matter rather of degree than of kind.

Paul Theroux, the author who was so hurt by V S Naipaul's sale of his copies of Theroux's novels inscribed to him that he wrote an entire book about his former friend's character, *Dr DeMarr*, at the heart of which is what one might call a meta-imposture.

George and Gerald DeMarr are identical twins who grow up hating one another because everyone treats them as interchangeable, as two limbs of one organism, as it were. They are therefore desperate to achieve their individuality, to lead separate and unique lives.

They do separate, until one day George turns up after many years at Gerald's house and asks for shelter. This Gerald reluctantly gives him, until about a week later he finds George dead from a heroin overdose. He disposes of his brother's body in the municipal waste site, thinking that in this way he has managed at long last to ensure his uniqueness.

This turns out not to be so, however. Gerald discovers that George was a doctor, and almost out of curiosity takes his place as such. George's qualifications, however, were bogus, that is to say forged: he specialised in treating hypochondriacs who, as Theroux puts it, wanted confirmation of their illness rather than cure. He also had a lucrative sideline in supplying prescriptions to drug addicts.

Unfortunately, Gerald, the impostor of an impostor, does not know how to write prescriptions; and while the hypochondriacs can be fobbed off with suggestions about diet, the drug addicts cannot be. They inject Gerald to death with heroin for not complying with their wishes, just as they injected George to death because he tried to break free of them; and so Gerald fails in his bid for uniqueness.

This is a disturbing little book, not least (for doctors) for its suggestion of how easily a completely untrained person may do so much of their work. Most disturbingly, it describes a world in which individuality does not develop spontaneously, has consciously to be worked at, and, precisely because it has to be worked at, will fail to develop. This is surely the world in which we now live, in which so many people resort to ornamental self mutilation in order to distinguish themselves from others, failing in the process precisely because there are so many others with exactly the same idea.

The gun what did it

Failure is the dark underbelly of success; for every outstanding case of the latter, there are many cases of the former. Perhaps that is why the US author and philosophical anarchist Henry David Thoreau wrote that most men lead lives of quiet desperation (and go to the grave with the song, if any, still in them). The necessity of failure for there ever to be success also explains why, in so optimistic a land as the United States, so much of the literature is tragic; the land of opportunity is also the land of missed opportunity. The study of failure is in any case a more fertile subject for literature than success; failure is both more various and attractive than success.

T Coraghessan (or T C) Boyle is a contemporary novelist and short story writer whose characters are often the failures who smoke, drink, take drugs, and rarely have satisfactory careers or marital relationships. They search but they do not find; they drift from disaster to disaster; a deep vein of self destruction lies in their character.

In the short story 'Killing Babies' the protagonist and narrator is a man who left school to join a rock group that broke up within a year, after which he drifted from job to job without ever finding a vocation. He drifted into a life of drink, drugs, and dishonesty; at the start of the story, he has just come out of drug rehabilitation (for the second time) and is going to stay with his older brother, the success of the family, a doctor in Detroit, who has given him a menial job in the laboratory of his clinic. It is hoped that this will keep him out of harm's way, on the straight and narrow path that leads from addiction.

He doesn't like his brother, who, at 38, is 10 years older than he. Greeting him at the airport after not having seen him for years, he says, 'You look like shit, Philip. You look like Dad just before he died—or maybe after he died.'

It turns out that his brother's clinic performs abortions and has attracted the attention of anti-abortion activists who picket it daily, singing hymns, shouting insults and slogans, and uttering menaces. Their self proclaimed love of human life does not preclude them from hating the staff of the clinic.

Life in a quiet Detroit suburb (this was before the city imploded) is not for the protagonist. He searches for, and soon finds, drugs:

I can see now that the Desoxyn [methamphetamine] was a mistake. It was exactly the kind of thing that they'd warned us about. But it wasn't coke and I just needed a lift, a buzz to work behind, and if he [the brother] did not want me to be tempted, then why had he left the key to the drug cabinet right there in the conch-shell ashtray on the corner of his desk?

This is a shrewd illustration of the tendency of addicts to blame others, or circumstances, for their conduct. He has a gun and, irritated by the aggressive and even violent self-righteousness of the anti-abortion protesters, he starts shooting them: 'It was easy. It was nothing. Just like killing babies. It is a regrettable fact that we often behave like, or worse than, those whom we most despise.'

A 13-year-old

Richard Hughes (1900-76) is now mainly remembered for his novel *A High Wind in Jamaica*, published in 1929, and for having been the friend of Dylan Thomas. Kingsley Amis and Philip Larkin made slighting reference to him in their correspondence, but that is no evidence of any bad qualities on his part.

Initially, however, Hughes wanted to be a dramatist, and it was as such that he first came to prominence. George Bernard Shaw called Hughes's first work, *The Sisters' Tragedy*, which he wrote aged 22 in 1922, the finest one act play ever written. It was produced at the Royal Court Theatre. Hughes went on two years later to write the first play in the world specifically for radio, called *Danger*.

The Sisters' Tragedy deals with the question of euthanasia. (Young men write surprisingly often about death, perhaps because it is for them of purely abstract interest and of no application to themselves.) Two sisters, Philippa, aged 28, and Charlotte, 19, devote themselves to looking after Owen, their 24 year old brother, who has a form of subacute sclerosing panencephalitis after measles, leaving him deaf, mute, and blind. Charlotte is engaged to marry but does not want to leave Philippa to look after Owen on her own.

There is a younger sister, too, called Lowrie, who is 13. She is at the stage of questioning everything, and the play begins after a pet rabbit has been savaged by the family cat and left alive but seriously injured and in terrible pain. Charlotte kills the rabbit; and of course Lowrie starts to ask questions as to whether it is sometimes right to kill. She is told that it is.

Lowrie draws the rather obvious but not quite accurate analogy between the rabbit and her brother. There is, for example, no evidence that Owen is actually suffering, whereas the rabbit was screaming after the cat attacked it. But Lowrie decides that it would be better for all concerned if Owen were dead: not only better for Owen himself but for her sister Charlotte, who would then be free to marry her fiancé.

There surely cannot be many plays in which a 13 year old is portrayed trying to strangle her severely disabled brother. Despite Lowrie's opinion that Owen would be better off dead, he fights back and makes it clear that he does not want to be strangled. Incapable of speech, though, he makes only what the family calls 'Owen's noise.'

Lowrie does not take the hint, however, but rather concludes that her method of euthanasia was a foolish one. She tries another method, this time successfully: she sends the blind Owen out for a walk, straight into the pond—which rather implausibly seems to abut immediately on to the French windows—knowing that he will drown in it, as he does.

Owen's death does not have the liberating effect on family life that Lowrie hoped for. After she has confessed that she virtually killed Owen, Charlotte's fiancé decides that he does not want to marry into a murderous family; instead he threatens to go to the police. As for Lowrie, she begins to hallucinate Owen, in a psychotic attempt to restore the status quo ante.

The play, incidentally, was written 11 years before J R Dawson proposed measles virus as the cause of subacute sclerosing panencephalitis.

Reality

Within a radius of a few miles of the hospital in which I worked were a number of what were once called dosshouses. (We laugh at the Victorians who supposedly covered up the erotically suggestive legs of pianos, but we routinely disguise realities with euphemisms.)

A certain specific kind of solidarity reigned in the dosshouses. The residents arranged for their social security payments to be paid on different days, so there was always money enough for the 3l bottles of strong cider that were their main interest in life, the lack of which would cause them acute suffering. But that was the only real solidarity they showed.

Reading Maxim Gorky's play *The Lower Depths*, first produced by the Moscow Arts Theatre in 1902, I am struck by how little has changed in the intervening century at this level of society. As in Gorky's day not all the inhabitants of the lower depths started life there: in the play one of the characters is an aristocrat, and the dosshouses I have visited often had a former lawyer or accountant.

In the second act of the play, one of the residents, Anna, who is 30 years old, dies, almost certainly from tuberculosis (from which Gorky himself suffered for much of his life, though it is more likely that he died by murder than from the disease). The other residents are unmoved by this.

Natasha: Have a look!
Bubnov: Look at what?
Natasha: Anna's dead!
Bubnov: That means she won't cough any more.

A few lines later Natasha says it's a good thing that Anna died but cannot help feeling sad. She wonders what sense there was in her life. Bubnov replies, 'It's like that with everybody. A man is born, lives a while and dies. I'll die too, and so will you. Nothing to be sad about.'

With Anna's body still present, Bubnov calls on the other resident to go sleep. The last line of the act before the curtain falls is spoken by another resident, Satin: 'Corpses don't hear, corpses don't feel. Shout, yell, corpses don't hear.'

The indifference shown is not an exaggeration. A dosshouse inhabitant once told me that he and his fellow residents, on finding one of their number dead in bed one day, did not know what to do about it and so went out drinking, their solution to all problems. They didn't tell anyone about the death for several days, preferring to sleep alongside the body than draw attention to it, as it didn't bother them.

Not even murder produces much of an effect. In the third act of *The Lower Depths* the keeper of the dosshouse, Kostylyov, is killed by a blow dealt by a young man, Peppel, during a quarrel. Satin tells him: 'Don't be afraid. Killing in a fight is no serious charge… I've punched the old man a few times myself. He didn't need much to keel over. Call me as a witness.'

In my career I've been called as a medical witness in several dosshouse murders. They could all have come out of Gorky's play: arbitrary, sudden, sordid, and drunken.

I'm not sure what conclusion to draw from the continuing accuracy of Gorky's play.

That people are irredeemably wicked?

That society is to blame?

Some combination of the two?

The problem with human existence is that it is so hard to comprehend.